SPRACHWISSENSCHAFTLICHE
STUDIENBÜCHER

WALTER SAUER

A Drillbook
of English Phonetics

Fifth Unrevised Edition

Universitätsverlag
WINTER
Heidelberg

Bibliografische Information der Deutschen Nationalbibliothek
Die Deutsche Nationalbibliothek verzeichnet diese Publikation
in der Deutschen Nationalbibliografie;
detaillierte bibliografische Daten sind im Internet
über *http://dnb.d-nb.de* abrufbar.

ISBN 978-3-8253-5216-5
5. Auflage 2020

Dieses Werk einschließlich aller seiner Teile ist urheberrechtlich geschützt. Jede Verwertung außerhalb der engen Grenzen des Urheberrechtsgesetzes ist ohne Zustimmung des Verlages unzulässig und strafbar.
Das gilt insbesondere für Vervielfältigungen, Übersetzungen,
Mikroverfilmungen und die Einspeicherung und Verarbeitung in elektronischen Systemen.

© 1979, 1990 Universitätsverlag C. Winter GmbH Heidelberg
© 2006, 2013, 2020 Universitätsverlag Winter GmbH Heidelberg
Imprimé en Allemagne · Printed in Germany
Druck: Memminger MedienCentrum, 87700 Memmingen

Gedruckt auf umweltfreundlichem, chlorfrei gebleichtem
und alterungsbeständigem Papier

Den Verlag erreichen Sie im Internet unter:
www.winter-verlag.de

CONTENTS

0	Preface	7
01	Abbreviations	12
02	Phonetic Symbols	13
03	The Organs of Speech	14
04	English Consonant Chart	15
05	English Vowel Charts	16
06	Main Features of RP Consonants	17
07	Main Features of RP Monophthongs	17
08	Selected Bibliography	18

Part I: PRONUNCIATION PRACTICE

1	Major Weak Forms	21
2	Plosives /p, t, k, b, d, g/	26
3	Approximant /r/	32
4	Fricatives /s, z, θ, ð/	36
5	Fricatives /f, v/	42
6	Approximant /w/	44
7	Approximant /j/	48
8	Lateral /l/	50
9	Fricatives /ʃ, ʒ/	54
10	Affricates /tʃ, dʒ/	54
11	Fricative /h/	58
12	Nasals /m, n, ŋ/	58
13	Front Vowel /i:/	62
14	Front-Central Vowel /ɪ/	64
15	Front Vowel /e/	66
16	Front Vowel /æ/	68
17	Central Vowel /ʌ/	70
18	Central-Back Vowel /ɑ:/	72
19	Back Vowel /ɒ/	74
20	Back Vowel /ɔ:/	76
21	Central Vowel /ɜ:/	78
22	Central Vowel /ə/	80
23	Back-Central Vowel /ʊ/	82
24	Back Vowel /u:/	82
25	Closing Diphthong /eɪ/	86
26	Closing Diphthong /aɪ/	86

27	Closing Diphthong /ɔɪ/	88
28	Closing Diphthong /aʊ/	92
29	Closing Diphthong /əʊ/	94
30	Centring Diphthong /ɪə/	96
31	Centring Diphthong /eə/	98
32	Centring Diphthong /ʊə/	98
33	Word Stress	104

Part II: TRANSCRIPTION PRACTICE

34–63. Text Transcriptions and Puzzles 112–144

0 Preface

This book has been compiled to accompany lecture courses on English phonetics and language laboratory classes in English pronunciation at university level. It is equally suitable for use as a self-instructional programme. With "cognitive learning" as its didactic concept, the *Drillbook* intends to teach English pronunciation by means of practical exercises as well as insights into underlying phonological structures and rules. It takes as its basis the predominant speech patterns of educated speakers of Southern English, commonly referred to as Received Pronunciation.

The programme presented in PART I focuses on pronunciation problems especially critical for German speakers, as suggested by a contrastive analysis of the phonological systems of the two languages and common teaching experience. The programme's comprehensiveness in dealing with problem areas of English pronunciation should, however, guarantee equal benefit to native speakers of other languages.

In general, the sequence of phonemes has been determined by considerations of related difficulties and pedagogical effectiveness, rather than by strict adherence to their phonetic classification. Reflecting students' frequent initial difficulties with English connected speech, the practice of Weak Forms in Chapter 1 precedes the treatment of individual phonemes. Each following chapter begins with articulation drills on its particular phoneme(s) and major allophones. For pedagogical purposes as well as reasons of space, phoneme variants aurally less noticeable and/or less problematic to produce have been omitted (e.g. unreleased final plosives, partially devoiced /r,l,w,j/, dental /n/ etc.), while some problems have deliberately been simplified. Further sections of each chapter deal with intensive practice of minimal or contrasting pairs, frequently mispronounced words or phoneme sequences. The Drill Sentences concluding the chapters have been put together so as to illustrate the occurrence of the phonemes and problem words in a natural colloquial context, with the occasional inclusion of short poems, nursery rhymes, tonguetwisters, dialogues and prose passages.

All the material in PART I has been recorded on two cassettes (160 minutes) for use in the language laboratory. One or more chapters can form the basis of a single laboratory session, depending on their length and level of difficulty, as well as the time available.

Concise phonetic background information, especially on the nature and distribution of specific allophones, can be found in the right hand margin. The abbreviations and formulae used have been adopted from current works on phonology and are explained on page 12.

A phonetic transcription of all exercises is provided on the facing pages. It follows *EPD* (14th ed., 1977) notation and reproduces the pronunciation of the speakers on tape, who conform to *EPD* standards. Possible RP variants are not listed in this section. Stress marks (primary and secondary) are used in all polysyllabic words, whereas sentences are marked with a simplified stress system (main stresses only).

Lack of space and time available in one semester demand that special chapters on intonation be omitted from this book. Adequate coverage of intonation problems is, however, indispensable and should be the subject of a separate course, perhaps using such an excellent approach as that in O'Connor and Arnold 1973.

PART II presents a number of model texts for phonetic transcription practice. As in the previous part orthographical text and phonetic script appear on facing pages. Variant pronunciations are cited in the footnotes, unless indicated within the word itself by parentheses. The texts have been transcribed in a natural RP style, allowing for occasional, though not necessarily consistent use of assimilations of the /kŋ gəʊ, dɪdʒʊ/-type. Weak forms and linking /r/ have been used whenever possible in order to underline typical patterns of connected English speech.

The puzzles contained in PART II combine easy exercises in phonetic transcription with such notoriously knotty problems as /s/ or /z/ and /θ/ or /ð/, or the pronunciation of proper and place names. Solutions are found on pages 142 ff. It is to be hoped that pleasure as well as profit will be derived from this lighter side of English phonetics.

To the Student

What scale-playing and music theory is to the piano student, the systematic study and continued practice of pronunciation is to the student of any foreign language. This *Drillbook* is designed to assist you in acquiring a good, i.e. "near native" English pronunciation. In pursuing this goal, you should consider these three points as being equally important:

1. *CAREFUL LISTENING.* An accurate ear for the fine points in English speech is indispensable to anyone wishing to speak the language with a good accent. Conscious and repeated listening will help you discriminate English sounds correctly and develop a critical ear.

2. *ACCURATE REPRODUCTION.* In imitating native English speakers, you should aim at closest approximation to what you hear. Remember, a Beethoven sonata may still be recognizable when played by an incompetent beginner, but it will give no pleasure to the audience. As a student of English, you should not be satisfied with minimal standards of intelligibility.

3. *INTELLIGENT PRACTICE.* Your English will only sound natural and "near native" once the patterns you use have become firmly established. Repeated − and repeated − practice (drilling) of the sounds in context will help you to habitualize their production in a way that makes them appear correct and spontaneous. You will, however, find drilling English pronunciation to be much less monotonous and considerably more efficient if you understand how and why the English sound system works as it does. This is why information on theoretical aspects of English phonetics forms an integral part of this book. Such a cognitive approach to language learning has proved to be the most rewarding.

Whether using this programme in a classroom situation, or practising English pronunciation individually, here are some hints to make your study more effective.

PART I: Before you start drilling a particular chapter, make sure you know what you are going to study. Review relevant passages of your lecture notes and/or read one (or more) of the suggested readings. Compare this material with the abbreviated phonetic background information in the right hand margin and make sure you understand the structure of the chapter. Read the text in phonetic script (or even better: transcribe it yourself and compare) and ask yourself why a particular word appears in a particular section or what the difficulty of a particular sentence may be. Note any surprises and potential problems. If you come across what you may consider an unusual pronunciation, consult the *EPD* to find out whether an acceptable variant pronunciation exists. Finally, although this is not strictly part of this book's objective, looking up the meanings of any unfamiliar words would provide an easy way of expanding your English vocabulary, besides making the drills − in the true sense of the word − more meaningful.

Your work in the language laboratory or with your own cassette recorder will follow a two-phase drill method ("Listen and repeat"). The cassettes accompanying this book will serve as your model. All words and sentences to be practised are printed in italics. An asterisk in the orthographic text indicates the end of a particular stimulus, after which space is provided for your response. Each chapter is divided into different sections. When working in the language laboratory, it is suggested that you break up a lesson into these sections, rewinding your tape at every ■ sign in order to check your performance against the model and correct any inaccuracies you might hear. Above all, you should not be satisfied with a single coverage of the material; remember that while listening is a necessary part of this programme, active speech practice is far more important. Frequent reference to the phonetic spelling of the spoken text will be especially helpful, since it can reinforce the aural stimulus through the visual medium.

PART II: When practising phonetic transcription, you should not only aim at mastering the skill of writing English in a phonemic alphabet − there are more exciting things in life − but consider such an exercise as a helpful tool towards acquiring a better English pronunciation. The items should be transcribed, with the model text covered, and closely compared with the transcription given. Repeated exercise will reduce the number of mistakes.

You will find that the puzzles contained in this section can provide entertainment, challenge your oral competence, as well as give you an opportunity to practise transcription skills. An additional hint: instead of turning to the solutions right away when you are stuck, refer to the *EPD* for help.

This *Drillbook* tries to make the learning of English phonetics and pronunciation as easy and pleasant as possible, but a certain amount of dedication and hard work is necessary. The texts and cassettes which make up this course provide you with all the basic material you need. The rest is up to you.

Acknowledgements

In a publication like the present *Drillbook* the debt to previous writers on English phonetics and phonology is obviously very great and is hereby gratefully acknowledged. I also wish to thank several of my colleagues and students for their suggestions and corrections. Thanks are due to Alison Rushworth, B.A. (London) and David McPherson Young, B.A. (Oxon.), whose voices appear on the tapes, and to Herbert Wahl, who supervised the recordings made at the Language Laboratory of Heidelberg University, whose authorities kindly permitted use of their facilities. Considerable help has come from my wife Nadine.

Grateful acknowledgement is made to the following authors and/or publishers for permission to reprint extracts from their publications:

New English Bible, Second Edition. (c)1970 by Permission of Oxford and Cambridge University Presses [45].

B. Shaw, *Pygmalion* (The Society of Authors, London) [47].

J. R. R. Tolkien, *The Hobbit* (London: Georg Allen & Unwin, ³1966) [49].

R. Galton and Simpson, A., *Hancock's Half Hour* (London: The Woburn Press, 1974) [53].

M. F. Wakelin, *English Dialects: An Introduction* (London: The Athlone Press of the University of London, ²1977) [55].

A. C. Gimson, *An Introduction to the Pronunciation of English* (London: Edward Arnold, ²1970 [56].

J. Lyons, *Introduction to Theoretical Linguistics* (Cambridge: Cambridge University Press, 1971) [59].

K. L. Pike, *Phonemics: A Technique for Reducing Languages to Writing* (Ann Arbor: The University of Michigan Press, 1947) [60].

0 1 Abbreviations

affr.	affricate
asp.	aspiration
aux.	auxiliary
C	consonant
dev-d	devoiced
diphth.	diphthongized
FC	Fortis consonant
gen.	genitive
homorg.	homorganic
LC	Lenis consonant
lat.	lateral
length.	lengthened
mod.	modal
n.	noun
nas.	nasal
neg.	negated
pa. t.	past tense
part.	partially
pl.	plural
plos.	plosive
pp.	past participle
pr.	present
sg.	singular
short.	shortened
v	voiced sound (LC or V)
v.	verb
V	vowel
v-d	voiced
/ /	phoneme
{ }	morpheme
/	in the context:
____	phoneme(s) in question
#	word boundary
■	Rewind, listen and correct
ˈ	stressed syllable
ˌ	secondary stress
·	unstressed syllable
*	repeat
→	can be realized as
[ ]	phonetic transcription
< >	spelling
~	usually
A-H	Arnold and Hansen 1989
CPD	Concise Pronouncing Dictionary
EPD	English Pronouncing Dictionary
G	Gimson 1989
S-W	Scherer and Wollmann 1986

0 2 Phonetic Symbols*

Each symbol is pronounced like the underlined letter(s) in the corresponding example.

Symbol	Example	Symbol	Example
Monophthongs:		Diphthongs:	
/ɪ/	fill	/aɪ/	file
/i:/	feel	/eɪ/	fail
/e/	fell	/ɔɪ/	foil
/æ/	cat	/aʊ/	foul
/ʌ/	cut	/əʊ/	foal
/ɑ:/	cart	/ɪə/	shear
/ɒ/	cot	/eə/	share
/ɔ:/	court	/ʊə/	sure
/ʊ/	full		
/u:/	fool		
/ə/	the		
/ɜ:/	third		

Consonants:

/p/	pig	/b/	big
/t/	tart	/d/	dart
/k/	curl	/g/	girl
/f/	file	/v/	vile
/s/	seal	/z/	zeal
/ʃ/	ruche	/ʒ/	rouge
/θ/	thigh	/ð/	thy
/tʃ/	chin	/dʒ/	gin
/m/	whim		
/n/	win		
/ŋ/	wing		
/w/	wail		
/h/	hail		
/j/	Yale		
/r/	rate		
/l/	late		

* Symbols used in this book are consistent with those in Daniel Jones, *Everyman's English Pronouncing Dictionary*. Rev. and ed. by A. C. Gimson; with revisions and Supplement by S. Ramsaran (London: Dent, [14]1988).

0 3 The Organs of Speech

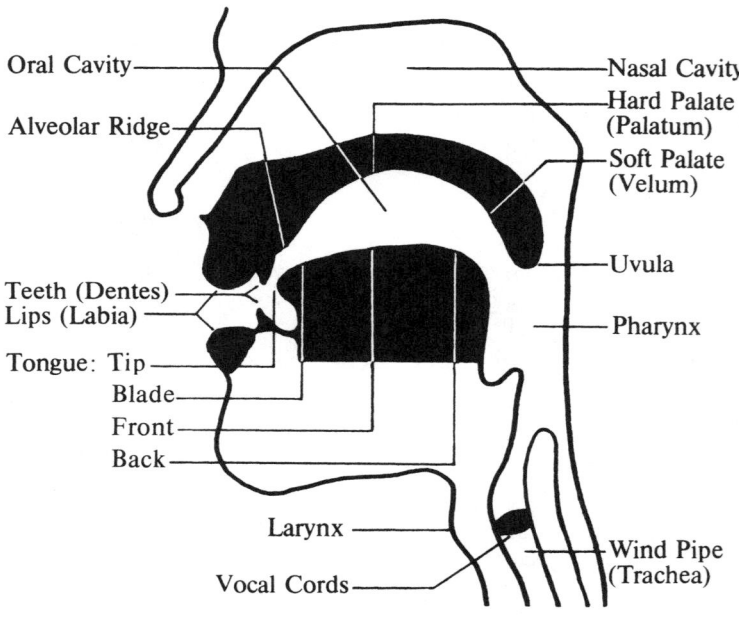

0 4 English Consonant Chart

point of articulation / manner of articulation	Bilabial	Labio-Dental	Dental	Alveolar	Post-Alveolar	Palato-Alveolar	Palatal	Velar	Glottal
Plosive	p b			t d				k g	
Fricative		f v	θ ð	s z		ʃ ʒ			h
Affricate						tʃ dʒ			
Nasal	m			n				ŋ	
Lateral				l					
Approximant/Semi-vowel	w				r		j		

0 5 English Vowel Charts

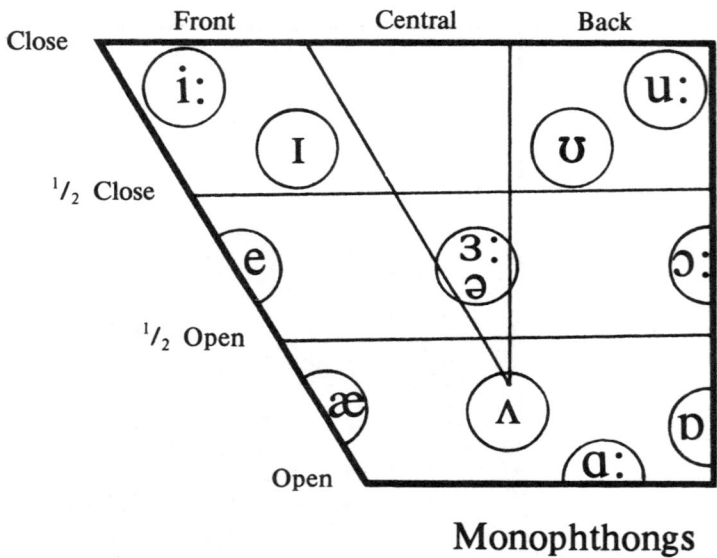

Monophthongs

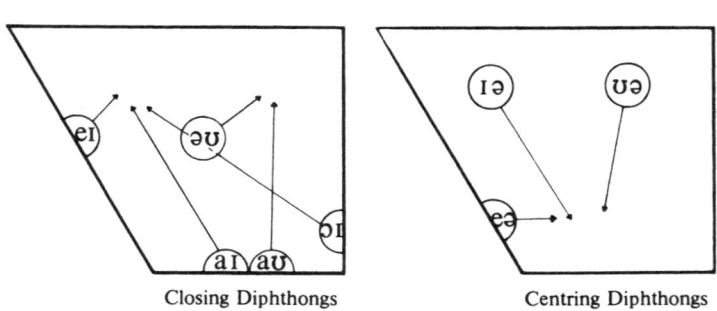

Closing Diphthongs

Centring Diphthongs

0 6 Main Features of RP Consonants

Phonemic (distinctive) features			Allophonic features
/p/	plosive,	bilabial,	fortis	aspiration; release
/t/	plosive,	alveolar,	fortis	aspiration; release
/k/	plosive,	velar,	fortis	aspiration; release
/b/	plosive,	bilabial,	lenis	voicing; release
/d/	plosive,	alveolar,	lenis	voicing; release
/g/	plosive,	velar,	lenis	voicing; release
/f/	fricative,	labio-dental,	fortis	-------
/θ/	fricative,	dental,	fortis	-------
/s/	fricative,	alveolar,	fortis	-------
/ʃ/	fricative,	palato-alveolar,	fortis	-------
/v/	fricative,	labio-dental,	lenis	voicing
/ð/	fricative,	dental,	lenis	voicing
/z/	fricative,	alveolar,	lenis	voicing
/ʒ/	fricative,	palato-alveolar,	lenis	voicing
/h/	fricative,	glottal,	(fortis)	-------
/tʃ/	affricate,	palato-alveolar,	fortis	-------
/dʒ/	affricate,	palato-alveolar,	lenis	voicing
/m/	nasal,	bilabial,	(lenis)	-------
/n/	nasal,	alveolar,	(lenis)	-------
/ŋ/	nasal,	velar,	(lenis)	-------
/l/	lateral,	alveolar,	(lenis)	voicing; resonance
/w/	approximant,	bilabial		voicing
/r/	approximant,	post-alveolar		voicing
/j/	approximant,	palatal		voicing

0 7 Main Features of RP Monophthongs

/i:/	Front vowel,	close,	lips unrounded
/ɪ/	Front-central vowel,	$\frac{1}{2}$ close,	lips unrounded
/e/	Front vowel,	$\frac{1}{2}$ close $-$ $\frac{1}{2}$ open,	lips unrounded
/æ/	Front vowel,	$\frac{1}{2}$ open, $-$ open,	lips unrounded
/ɑ:/	Central-back vowel,	open,	lips unrounded
/ɒ/	Back vowel,	open,	lips rounded
/ɔ:/	Back vowel,	$\frac{1}{2}$ open $-$ $\frac{1}{2}$ close,	lips rounded
/ʊ/	Back-central vowel,	$\frac{1}{2}$ close,	lips rounded
/u:/	Back vowel,	close,	lips rounded
/ʌ/	Central vowel,	$\frac{1}{2}$ open $-$ open,	lips unrounded
/ɜ:/	Central vowel,	$\frac{1}{2}$ close $-$ $\frac{1}{2}$ open,	lips unrounded
/ə/	Central vowel, (unaccented)	($\frac{1}{2}$ close $-$) $\frac{1}{2}$ open,	lips unrounded

0 8 Selected Bibliography

Arnold, R. and K. Hansen (^{10}1996), *Englische Phonetik*. Leipzig: Langenscheid.

Carr, Philip (^{3}2013), *English Phonetics and Phonology*. An Introduction. Chichester: Wiley-Blackwell.

Colins, Beverley and Inger M. Mees (^{3}2013), *Practical Phonetics and Phonology: A Resource Book for Students*. Abingdon: Routledge.

Cruttenden, Alan (^{6}2001), *Gimson's Pronunciation of English*. London: Arnold.

Davis, J.F. (1998), *Phonetics and Phonology*. Stuttgart: Klett.

Jones, Daniel (^{9}1976), *An Outline of English Phonetics*. Cambridge: Cambridge University Press.

Jones, D. (^{18}2011), *Cambridge English Pronouncing Dictionary*. (Edited by Peter Roach, Jane Setter & John Esling.) Cambridge: Cambridge University Press.

O'Connor, J.D. and G.F. Arnold (^{3}1973), *Intonation of Colloquial English: A Practical Handbook*. London: Longman.

Olausson, Lena and Catherine Sangster (2006), *Oxford BBC Guide to Pronunciation*. Oxford: Oxford University Press.

Pointon, G.E. (ed.), (^{2}1990), *BBC Pronouncing Dictionary of British Names*. Oxford: Oxford University Press.

Scherer, G. and A. Wollmann (^{3}1986), *Englische Phonetik und Phonologie*. Grundlagen der Anglistik und Amerikanistik 6. Berlin: Schmidt.

Wells, J.C. (^{3}2008), *Longman Pronunciation Dictionary*. Harlow: Longman.

PART I
PRONUNCIATION PRACTICE

1 Major Weak Forms

1 1 Listen to the following extract from *Alice in Wonderland*. Do not read along the printed text.

Alice was *beginning* to *get very tired* of *sitting by* her *sister on* the *bank,* and of *having nothing* to *do: once or twice* she had *peeped in*to the *book* her *sister* was *reading,* but *it had no pictures or conversations in it,* "and *what* is the *use* of a *book,*" *thought Alice, "without pictures or conversations?"*

So she was *considering, in* her *own mind* (as *well* as she *could,* for the *hot day made* her *feel very sleepy* and *stupid), whether* the *pleasure* of *making* a *daisychain* would be *worth* the *trouble* of *getting up* and *picking* the *daisies, when suddenly* a *white rabbit with pink eyes ran close by* her.

There was *nothing so very remarkable in that; nor did Alice think it so very much out* of the *way* to *hear* the *Rabbit say* to *itself, "Oh dear! Oh dear! I* shall be *too late!" (when* she *thought it over afterwards, it occurred* to *her* that she *ought* to have *wondered* at *this,* but at the *time it all seemed quite natural);* but *when* the *Rabbit actually took* a *watch out* of *its waistcoatpocket,* and *looked* at *it,* and *then hurried on, Alice started* to her *feet,* for *it flashed across* her *mind* that she had *never before seen* a *rabbit with either* a *waistcoat-pocket, or* a *watch* to *take out* of *it, and, burning with curiosity,* she *ran across* the *field after it,* and was *just in time* to *see it pop down* a *large rabbithole under* the *hedge.*

In another moment down went Alice after it, never once considering how in the *world* she was to *get out again.*

The rabbit-hole went straight on like a *tunnel* for *some way,* and *then dipped suddenly down, so suddenly* that *Alice had not* a *moment* to *think about stopping* her*self before* she *found* her*self falling down what seemed* to be a *very deep well.*

Either the *well* was *very deep, or* she *fell very slowly,* for she *had plenty* of *time* as she *went down* to *look about* her, and to *wonder what* was *going* to *happen next.*

1 2 Rewind and listen again. While following the printed text, pay special attention to the pronunciation of the non-italicized words (Weak Forms).

1 3 Weak Form (WF) Drills

	WF	Context
1 *Where* am *I going?* *	/əm/	/ ~
I'm awfully sorry. *	/m/	/aɪ___
2 *Six* and *six makes twelve.* *	/ən(d)/	/ ~
She cooked liver and *onions.* *		
3 *What* are *they doing?* *	/ə/	/___C
His sisters are *extremely nice.* *	/ər/	/___V
4 *She did it* as *well* as *she could.* *	/əz/	/ ~
This is twice as *far.* *		
5 *He found the book* at *the bookshop.* *	/ət/	/ ~
At *the time it all seemed natural.* *		
■		
6 *It seemed to* be *a deep well.* *	°/bɪ/	/ ~
I mustn't be *late.* *		
7 *I've never* been *so disgusted.* *	°/bɪn/	/ ~
Has Fred ever been *to London?* *		
8 *It never rains* but *it pours.* *	/bət/	/ ~
We cannot but *hope.* *		
9 *You* can *do what you like.* *	/k(ə)n/	/ ~
Where can *they be?* *		
10 *I* could *wring his neck for it.* *	°/k(ə)d/	/ ~
Who could *help me?* *		
■		
11 *What* do *they want?* *	/də/	/___C²
How do *I find out about it?* *	/dʊ/	/___V²
How do *you do?* *	/d/	/___jʊ²
12 *Who* does *he think he is?* *	/dəz/	/ ~ ²
When does *it begin?* *		
13 *This is asking* for *trouble.* *	/fə/	/___C
He bought it for *a pound.* *	/fər/	/___V
14 *She took down a jar* from *the shelf.* *	/frəm/	/ ~
They came from *all directions.* *		
15 *John* had *never seen it.* *	/(h)əd/¹	/C___²
She'd told him so many times. *	/d/	/V___²
■		

° Strong Form equally acceptable.
¹ Form with /h/ must be used after pause.
² Strong Form must be used for main verb.

		WF	Context
16	*Charles* has *done it.* *	/(h)əz/[1]	/s, z, ʃ, ʒ, tʃ, dʒ___[2]
	It's never *been tried before.* *	/s/	/FC___[2]
	Jane has *got a splendid idea.* *	/(h)(ə)z/	/LC___[2]
	He's brought *you a present.* *	/z/	/V___[2]
17	*What* have *you done?* *	/(h)əv/[1]	/C___[2]
	We've seen *the film.* *	/v/	/V___[2]
18	*Can* he *do no wrong?* *	°/(h)ɪ/[1]	/ ~ [3]
	It's better than he *thought.* *		
19	*Would you lend* her *your car?* *	°/(h)ə/[1]	/___C
	Let's give her *a hand.* *	°/(h)ər/[1]	/___V
20	*They didn't believe* him. *	/(h)ɪm/[1]	/ ~
	Show him *the castle.* *		
■			
21	*Philip likes* his *bike.* *	/(h)ɪz/[1]	/ ~
	Michael broke his *leg.* *		
22	*Reg* is *a nice boy.* *	/ɪz/	/s, z, ʃ, ʒ, tʃ, dʒ___
	What's the *time?* *	/s/	/FC___
	Nell is *always late.* *	/z/	/LC___
	He is *very hungry.* *	/z/	/V___
23	*Let* me *see.* *	°/mɪ/	/ ~
	Tell me *another story.* *		
24	*We* must *keep smiling.* *	/məs(t)/	/___C
	You must *always remember.* *	/məst/	/___V
25	*What is the use* of *a book?* *	/əv/	/___V
	How about a cup of *tea?* *	/ə(v)/	/___C
■			
26	*I spent two terms at* St. *Andrews.* *	/s(ə)nt/	/___V
	St. *George killed the dragon.* *	/s(ə)n(t)/	/___C
27	*I* shall *be too busy.* *	/ʃ(ə)l/	/ ~
	Where shall *we go?* *		
28	*She ran across the field.* *	°/ʃɪ/	/ ~ [3]
	He thought she *was older.* *		

[3] Strong Form must be used before /d/ (had, would), /z/ (has, is), /v/ (have), /l/ (will).

29 *I* should *think so.* * *He* should *know better.* *	°/ʃ(ə)d/	/ ~
30 *Could I borrow* some *money?* * *Would you like* some *tea?* * ■	/s(ə)m/	/ ~ ⁴
31 *Peter's older* than *Robert.* * *Better late* than *never.* *	/ðən/	/ ~
32 *This is the house* that *Jack built.* * *Don't tell me* that *you lost it.* *	/ðət/	/ ~ ⁵
33 *I can't stand* them. * *He wrote* them *a letter.* *	/ðəm/	/ ~
34 *There was nothing remarkable.* * *Isn't* there *any more cake?* * *There's no doubt about it.* *	/ðə/ /ðər/ /ðəz/	/___C⁵ /___V⁵ /there's⁵
35 *The Rabbit said* to *itself: "Oh dear!"* * *She tried* to *look down.* * ■	/tʊ/ /tə/	/___V,w /___C
36 *Did they invite* us? * *Let's* ask *him.* *	/əs/ /s/	/ ~ /let___
37 *Alice* was *beginning to get tired.* * *It* was *nothing unusual.* *	/wəz/	/ ~
38 *When do we have to leave?* * *We can easily find out.* *	°/wɪ/	/ ~ ³
39 *They* were *quite right.* * *The boxes* were *all open.* * ■	/wə/ /wər/	/___C /___V
40 *This is the chap* who *hit me.* * *Can you tell us* who *wrote this?* *	°/(h)ʊ/¹	/ ~ ³
41 *You'll never guess.* * *It* will *be fantastic.* *	/(wə)l/ /əl/	/V___ /C___
42 *I'd go if I could.* * *It* would *be very nice.* *	/d/ °/(w)əd/	/V___ /C___
43 *Serve you right.* * *You never can tell.* * ■	°/jʊ/	/ ~ ³

⁴ Weak Form can be used only when meaning "an unspecified number".
⁵ Strong Form must be used for demonstr. pron., adj., adv.

1 4 Weak Form (WF) or Strong Form (StF)?
Listen to the following dialogue in its entirety. Then drill each sentence separately.

A: Was *Mother surprised* that *I came?* *	WF	/ ~
B: *Yes. At least* that'*s what she told* us. *	StF StF	/accented
Anyway, what are you here for? *	StF	/before pause (except pronoun)
A: *Well, tomorrow's Mother's birthday, and I wanted to surprise* her. *	WF	/pronoun before pause
B: *Goodness, I* had*n't even remembered.* *	StF	/contracted neg. aux. or mod. v.
Could *you lend me some money?* *	StF or WF	/after pause before WF
I've got to buy a present for *her.* *	StF or WF	/prep. before pronoun before pause

■

2 Plosives /p, t, k, b, d, g/

2 1 Major Allophone Drills

	Allophone	Context

2 1 1 Fortes

	Allophone	Context
push, Pam, pass * *touch, tell, time* * *catch, came, chaos* *	full asp.	/___ 'V
happen, leper, supper * *auntie, eater, outing* * *liquor, socket, lichen* *	slight asp.	/___ .V
spin, spell, asparagus * *stock, astonish, stew* * *skill, sky, scheme* *	no asp.	/s___

∎

2 1 2 Lenes

	Allophone	Context
lobby, sober, amber * *Edda, alder, candy* * *logging, aghast, eager* *	fully v-d	/v___v
buy, bit, bush * *dash, doom, dean* * *gush, goof, game* *	part. dev-d	/#___
cab, knob, nib * *ad, lid, loud* * *hog, mug, snug* *	dev-d	/___#

∎

2 1 3 Fortes and Lenes

	Allophone	Context
a dead dog, soapbox, magpie * *object, a sick chick, lecture* *	no release	/___ plos. /___ affr.
at last, idol, beetle * *middle, settle, handle* *	lat. release (/t, d/)	/___ lat.
fatten, Edna, leaden * *shipment, submarine* *	nas. release (/t, d, p, b/)	/___ homorg. nas.

∎

2

2 1

2 1 1

puʃ, pæm, pɑːs
tʌtʃ, tel, taɪm
kætʃ, keɪm, ˈkeɪɒs
ˈhæpən, ˈlepə, ˈsʌpə
ˈɑːntɪ, ˈiːtə, ˈaʊtɪŋ
ˈlɪkə, ˈsɒkɪt, ˈlaɪkən
spɪn, spel, əˈspærəgəs
stɒk, əˈstɒnɪʃ, stjuː
skɪl, skaɪ, skiːm
■

2 1 2

ˈlɒbɪ, ˈsəʊbə, ˈæmbə
ˈedə, ˈɔːldə, ˈkændɪ
ˈlɒgɪŋ, əˈgɑːst, ˈiːgə
baɪ, bɪt, bʊʃ
dæʃ, duːm, diːn
gʌʃ, guːf, geɪm
kæb, nɒb, nɪb
æd, lɪd, laʊd
hɒg, mʌg, snʌg
■

2 1 3

ə ˈded ˈdɒg, ˈsəʊpbɒks, ˈmægpaɪ
ˈɒbdʒekt, ə ˈsɪk ˈtʃɪk, ˈlektʃə
ət ˈlɑːst, ˈaɪdl, ˈbiːtl
ˈmɪdl, ˈsetl, ˈhændl
ˈfætn, ˈednə, ˈledn
ˈʃɪpmənt, ˌsʌbməˈriːn
■

2 1 4 Dental /t, d/
    width, eighth, bad thoughts * /___ θ
    not these, get them * /___ ð
    ■

2 2 Minimal Pairs
    pull : *bull* * *tie* : *die* * *come* : *gum* *
    cap : *cab* * *late* : *laid* * *buck* : *bug* *
    sop : *sob* * *feet* : *feed* * *hack* : *hag* *
    nipple : *nibble* * *shutter* : *shudder* * *anchor* : *anger**
    ■

2 3 Pronunciation of < -ed > {pa.t.}, {pp.}

touched, passed, packed, laughed, nipped *	/t/	/FC (except t)___
sobbed, loved, buzzed, feared, sighed, snowed *	/d/	/LC (except d)___ /V___
ended, faded, fitted, waited *	/ɪd/	/d, t___

■

2 4 Pronunciation of < -ed > adjectives and < -edly > adverbs

an aged woman, blessed assurance * *a crooked road, a learned man* * *a wicked witch, a wretched girl* *	/ɪd/
advisedly, assuredly, confessedly * *deservedly, markedly, unfeignedly* *	/ɪdlɪ/

■

2 5 Some words with "silent plosives"
    < p, b > *cupboard, pneumonia, pneumatic* *
            Ptolemy, doubt, debt, subtle *
            climb, womb, plumber, combing *
    < t, d > *Christmas, mustn't, apostle* *
            Guildford, handkerchief, handsome *
    < k, g > *knight, knuckle, know* *
            gnaw, gnat, sign *
    ■

2 1 4

wɪdθ, eɪtθ, ˈbæd ˈθɔːts
ˈnɒt ˈðiːz, ˈget ðəm
■

2 2

pʊl : bʊl,   taɪ : daɪ,   kʌm : gʌm
kæp : kæb,   leɪt : leɪd,   bʌk : bʌg
sɒp : sɒb,   fiːt : fiːd,   hæk : hæg
ˈnɪpl : ˈnɪbl,   ˈʃʌtə : ˈʃʌdə,   ˈæŋkə : ˈæŋgə
■

2 3

tʌtʃt, pɑːst, pækt
lɑːft, nɪpt
sɒbd, lʌvd, bʌzd
fɪəd, saɪd, snəʊd
ˈendɪd, ˈfeɪdɪd, ˈfɪtɪd, ˈweɪtɪd
■

2 4

ən ˈeɪdʒɪd ˈwʊmən, ˈblesɪd əˈʃʊərəns
ə ˈkrʊkɪd ˈrəʊd, ə ˈlɜːnɪd mæn
ə ˈwɪkɪd ˈwɪtʃ, ə ˈretʃɪd ˈɡɜːl
ədˈvaɪzɪdlɪ, əˈʃʊərɪdlɪ, kənˈfesɪdlɪ
dɪˈzɜːvɪdlɪ, ˈmɑːkɪdlɪ, ʌnˈfeɪnɪdlɪ
■

2 5

ˈkʌbəd, njuːˈməʊnjə, njuːˈmætɪk
ˈtɒləmɪ, daʊt, det, ˈsʌtl
klaɪm, wuːm, ˈplʌmə, ˈkəʊmɪŋ
ˈkrɪsməs, ˈmʌsnt, əˈpɒsl
gɪlfəd, ˈhæŋkətʃɪf, ˈhænsəm
naɪt, ˈnʌkl, nəʊ
nɔː, næt, saɪn
■

2 6 Drill Sentences

1 *Don't panic!* *
2 *The dog can't bite.* *
3 *Saturday is payday.* *
4 *Shut up, Steve.* *
5 *I'm fed up with your constant talking.* *

∎

6 *Ted tiptoed in the dark.* *
7 *Spit it out, Peter, stop hiccoughing.* *
8 *Let's put all the eggs in one basket.* *
9 *Did you get it at all?* *
10 *Go get them, tiger!* *

∎

11 *This handbag is not too big.* *
12 *Eight days ago the Thames was badly flooded.* *
13 *Babies like to play pat-a-cake.* *
14 *Wasn't it odd that the last two bottles were empty?* *
15 *Betty Botter bought some butter.* *

∎

16 *Stephanie's speciality is the scholarly study of Connecticut.* *
17 *Lab techniques can be learned at most state schools.* *
18 *Thomas spent most of his time in pubs.* *
19 *Towards the middle of winter, I lost my job.* *
20 *Peter Piper picked a peck of pickled peppers;*
   A peck of pickled peppers Peter Piper picked;
   If Peter Piper picked a peck of pickled peppers,
   Where's the peck of pickled peppers Peter Piper picked? *

∎

2 6

1. ˈdəʊnt ˈpænɪk.
2. ðə ˈdɒg kɑːnt ˈbaɪt.
3. ˈsætədeɪ ɪz ˈpeɪdeɪ.
4. ˈʃʌt ˈʌp, ˈstiːv.
5. aɪm ˈfed ˈʌp wɪð jɔː ˈkɒnstənt ˈtɔːkɪŋ.

■

6. ˈted ˈtɪptəʊd ɪn ðə ˈdɑːk.
7. ˈspɪt ɪt ˈaʊt, ˈpiːtə, ˈstɒp ˈhɪkʌpɪŋ.
8. lets pʊt ˈɔːl ðɪ ˈegz ɪn ˈwʌn ˈbɑːskɪt.
9. dɪd ju ˈget ɪt ət ˈɔːl?
10. ˈgəʊ ˈget ðəm, ˈtaɪgə!

■

11. ˈðɪs ˈhændbæg ɪz nɒt ˈtuː ˈbɪg.
12. ˈeɪt ˈdeɪz əˈgəʊ ðə ˈtemz wəz ˈbædlɪ ˈflʌdɪd.
13. ˈbeɪbɪz ˈlaɪk tə ˈpleɪ ˈpætəkeɪk.
14. ˈwɒznt ɪt ˈɒd ðət ðə ˈlɑːst tuː ˈbɒtlz wər ˈemptɪ?
15. ˈbetɪ ˈbɒtə ˈbɔːt səm ˈbʌtə.

■

16. ˈstefənɪz speʃɪˈælətɪ ɪz ðə ˈskɒləlɪ ˈstʌdɪ əv kəˈnetɪkət.
17. ˈlæb tekˈniːks kən bɪ ˈlɜːnd ət ˈməʊst steɪt ˈskuːlz.
18. ˈtɒməs spent ˈməʊst əv hɪz ˈtaɪm ɪn ˈpʌbz.
19. tʊˈwɔːdz ðə ˈmɪdl əv ˈwɪntə, aɪ ˈlɒst maɪ ˈdʒɒb.
20. ˈpiːtə ˈpaɪpə ˈpɪkt ə ˈpek əv ˈpɪkld ˈpepəz;
    ə ˈpek əv ˈpɪkld ˈpepəz ˈpiːtə ˈpaɪpə ˈpɪkt;
    ɪf ˈpiːtə ˈpaɪpə ˈpɪkt ə ˈpek əv ˈpɪkld ˈpepəz,
    ˈweəz ðə ˈpek əv ˈpɪkld ˈpepəz ˈpiːtə ˈpaɪpə ˈpɪkt?

■

3   Approximant /r/

3 1   Major Allophone Drills

	Allophone	Context
3 1 1 *wrist, rock, rigorous* * *Rome, race, rude* * *rhododendron, roaring, rhinoceros* * *refrigerator, rhetoric, rigmarole* * ■	v-d	/ ~
3 1 2 *proud, practice, priest* * *trade, trick, attractive* * *crib, crest, Christ* * ■	dev-d	/p, t, k ___'V (except sp, st, sk)

3 1 3   Contrast:

trill : drill *   *trout : drought* *   *trawler : drawler* *
pride : bride *   *prude : brood* *   *preach : breach* *
crate : great *   *cram : gramme* *   *crowned : ground* *
■

3 2   Free Variant: "flapped /r/" (optional)

hurry, carry, period * *sorry, very, bury* *	/V___V
three, through, thresh, thread *	/θ___
brethren, with regret * ■	/ð___

3 3   Distribution of /r/
3 3 1   /r/

repeat, rural, Paris, stretch *   /___V

3 3 2   "Silent r"

fear, Peter, car * *boar, motor, caviar* *	/<r>#
cart, lord, earl * *bird, earn, stark* * ■	/<r>C

3

3 1

3 1 1
rɪst, rɒk, ˈrɪɡərəs
rəʊm, reɪs, ruːd
ˌrəʊdəˈdendrən, ˈrɔːrɪŋ, raɪˈnɒsərəs
rɪˈfrɪdʒəreɪtə, ˈretərɪk, ˈrɪɡmərəʊl
■

3 1 2
praʊd, ˈpræktɪs, priːst
treɪd, trɪk, əˈtræktɪv
krɪb, krest, kraɪst
■

3 1 3
trɪl : drɪl,   traʊt : draʊt,   ˈtrɔːlə : ˈdrɔːlə
praɪd : braɪd, pruːd : bruːd, priːtʃ : briːtʃ
kreɪt : ɡreɪt, kræm : ɡræm,   kraʊnd : ɡraʊnd
■

3 2
ˈhʌrɪ, ˈkærɪ, ˈpɪərɪəd
ˈsɒrɪ, ˈverɪ, ˈberɪ
θriː, θruː, θreʃ, θred
ˈbreðrən, wɪð rɪˈɡret
■

3 3

3 3 1
rɪˈpiːt, ˈrʊərəl, ˈpærɪs, stretʃ

3 3 2
fɪə, ˈpiːtə, kɑː
bɔː, ˈməʊtə, ˈkævɪɑː
kɑːt, lɔːd, ɜːl
bɜːd, ɜːn, stɑːk
■

3 3 3 "Linking /r/"

    tear it, car engine, fire exit *　　　　　　　　　　/___#V*
    Sir Adam, never again, poor Aunt *

3 3 4 Contrast:

    for nothing : *for a trifle* *　　*a bar* : *a bar of soap* *
    our hope : *our only hope* *　　*my sister* : *my sister Anne* *
    rear : *rear end* *　　*solar* : *solar energy* *

3 3 5 "Intrusive /r/" (optional)

    China and the U.S., the idea of doing it *　　　/ə___#V
    the Shah of Persia, draw out, law and order *　/ɑː, ɔː___#V
    ■

3 4 Drill Sentences

    1 *Right or wrong, my country.* *
    2 *Cheer up, Ronald, give it a try.* *
    3 *Canterbury has a very remarkable cathedral.* *
    4 *This programme is really atrocious.* *
    5 *Brian's secretary is a dreadfully boring character.* *

    ■

    6 *Row, row, row your boat gently down the stream,*
       Merrily, merrily, merrily, merrily, life is but a dream. *
    7 *The waitress tripped and dropped a tray.* *
    8 *The children lived happily ever after.* *
    9 *Rule, Britannia! Britannia, rule the waves;*
       Britons never, never, never shall be slaves. *

    ■

    10 Listen to the following dialogue in its entirety. Then drill each sentence separately.

        A: *Are you still planning a trip to Great Britain this spring, Rosemary?* *
        B: *I don't think so, Richard.* * *Doris and I want to spend April in Paris in order to brush up our French.* *
        A: *Will you have a travel bureau arrange your reservations?* * *Paris can be terribly crowded at that time of year.* *
        B: *Yes.* * *My brother has promised to take care of everything.* * *I'm really grateful for that.* *

3 3 3

'teər ıt, 'kɑːr 'endʒın, 'faıər 'eksıt
sər 'ædəm, 'nevər ə'gen, 'pʊər 'ɑːnt

3 3 4

fə 'nʌθıŋ : fər ə 'traıfl,   ə 'bɑː : ə 'bɑːr əv 'səʊp
'ɑː 'həʊp : 'ɑːr 'əʊnlı 'həʊp,   maı 'sıstə : maı 'sıstər 'æn
rıə : 'rıər 'end,   'səʊlə : 'səʊlər 'enədʒı

3 3 5

'tʃaınər ənd ðə 'juː 'es, ðı aı'dıər əv 'duːıŋ ıt,
ðə 'ʃɑːr əv 'pɜːʃə, 'drɔːr 'aʊt, 'lɔːr ənd 'ɔːdə

∎

3 4

1 'raıt ɔː 'rɒŋ, maı 'kʌntrı.
2 'tʃıər 'ʌp, 'rɒnəld, 'gıv ıt ə 'traı.
3 'kæntəbrı hæz ə 'verı rı'mɑːkəbl kə'θiːdrəl.
4 'ðıs 'prəʊgræm ız 'rıəlı ə'trəʊʃəs.
5 'braıənz 'sekrətrı ız ə 'dredfəlı 'bɔːrıŋ 'kærəktə.

∎

6 'rəʊ, 'rəʊ, 'rəʊ jɔː 'bəʊt 'dʒentlı 'daʊn ðə 'striːm,
   'merılı, 'merılı, 'merılı, 'merılı, 'laıf ız 'bʌt ə 'driːm.
7 ðə 'weıtrəs 'trıpt ən 'drɒpt ə 'treı.
8 ðə 'tʃıldrən lıvd 'hæpılı 'evər 'ɑːftə.
9 'ruːl, brı'tænjə! brı'tænjə 'ruːl ðə 'weıvz;
   'brıtənz 'nevə, 'nevə, 'nevə 'ʃæl bı 'sleıvz.

∎

10

eıː : ɑː juː 'stıl 'plænıŋ ə 'trıp tə 'greıt 'brıtn ðıs 'sprıŋ, 'rəʊzmərı?
biː : aı dəʊnt 'θıŋk 'səʊ, 'rıtʃəd. 'dɒrıs ənd 'aı 'wɒnt tə 'spend 'eıprəl ın 'pærıs ın 'ɔːdə tə 'brʌʃ 'ʌp aʊə 'frenʃ.
eıː : wıl juː hæv ə 'trævl 'bjʊərəʊ ə'reındʒ jɔː rezə'veıʃnz? 'pærıs kəm bı 'terıblı 'kraʊdıd ət 'ðæt 'taım əv 'jıə.
biː : 'jes. maı 'brʌðəz 'prɒmıst tə 'teık 'keər əv 'evrıθıŋ. aım 'rıəlı 'greıtfʊl fə 'ðæt.

35

A: *I thought you wanted to do some research in the University Library at Cambridge.* * *Or have you already written your paper on children's literature?* *

B: *I'm afraid I haven't.* * *But Doris isn't too interested in prose, drama or poetry, and Britain isn't her favourite country either.* * *So we decided to compromise.* * *After all, I'll probably find the right material here in our library.* *

A: *Sorry I'm in rather a hurry.* * *I'm off to a history lecture on the Russian Revolution by Professor Brook.* * *Cheerio.* *

■

4 Fricatives /s, z, θ, ð/

4 1 Articulation Drills (Fortes)
4 1 1 /s/
sick, facing, yes *
sand, crescent, goose *
sun, newspaper, house *

4 1 2 /θ/
thick, method, earth *
theme, author, cloth *
thirst, catholic, faith *
■

4 2 Major Allophone Drills (Lenes)

	Allophone	Context
4 2 1 /z/		
busy, freezer, raising * *housing, wizard, resolve* *	fully v-d	/v___v
zipper, zero, zodiac * *Zambia, zucchini, Zoe* *	part. dev-d	/#___
because, choose, fuse * *furs, wise, pause* *	dev-d	/___#

■

eɪ: : aɪ 'θɔ:t jʊ 'wɒntɪd tə 'du: səm rɪsɜ:tʃ ɪn ðə ju:nɪ'vɜ:sətɪ 'laɪbrɪ ət 'keɪmbrɪdʒ. ɔ: 'hæv jʊ ɔ:l redɪ 'rɪtn jɔ: 'peɪpər ɒn 'tʃɪldrənz 'lɪtrətʃə?

bi: : aɪm ə'freɪd aɪ 'hævnt. bət 'dɒrɪs ɪznt tu: 'ɪntrestɪd ɪn 'prəʊz, 'drɑ:mər ɔ: 'pəʊətrɪ, ənd 'brɪtn 'ɪznt hə 'feɪvrɪt 'kʌntrɪ 'aɪðə. səʊ wɪ dɪ'saɪdɪd tə 'kɒmprəmaɪz. ɑ:ftər 'ɔ:l, aɪl 'prɒbəblɪ 'faɪnd ðə 'raɪt mə'tɪərɪəl hɪər ɪn 'aʊə 'laɪbrərɪ.

eɪ: : 'sɒrɪ aɪm ɪn 'rɑ:ðər ə 'hʌrɪ. aɪm 'ɒf tʊ ə 'hɪstrɪ 'lektʃər ɒn ðə 'rʌʃn revə'lu:ʃn baɪ prə'fesə 'brʊk. 'tʃɪərɪəʊ.

■

4

4 1
4 1 1

sɪk, 'feɪsɪŋ, jes
sænd, 'kresnt, gu:s
sʌn, 'nju:speɪpə, haʊs

4 1 2

θɪk, 'meθəd, ɜ:θ
θi:m, 'ɔ:θə, klɒθ
θɜ:st, 'kæθəlɪk, feɪθ

■

4 2

4 2 1

'bɪzɪ, 'fri:zə, 'reɪzɪŋ
'haʊzɪŋ, 'wɪzəd, rɪ'zɒlv
'zɪpə, 'zɪərəʊ, 'zəʊdɪæk
'zæmbɪə, zʊ'ki:nɪ, 'zəʊɪ
brɪ'kɒz, tʃu:z, ʃu:z
fɜ:z, waɪz, pɔ:z

■

4 2 2 /ð/

	Allophone	Context
heather, other, bother *	fully v-d	/v___v
further, leather, heathen *		
though, that, this *	part. dev-d	/#___
their, these, thine *		
tithe, loathe, breathe *	dev-d	/___#
lathe, clothe, blithe *		

■

4 3 Minimal Pairs

sink : zinc *   Sue : zoo* *   seal : zeal* *
bussing : buzzing *   precedent : President* *   fussy : fuzzy* *
cease : seize *   dice : dies* *   price : prize* *
thigh : thy *
ether : either *
wreath : wreathe *   teeth : teethe* *   mouth : mouth* (v.)
sum : thumb *   sane : thane* *   saw : thaw* *
miss : myth *   moss : moth* *   force : fourth* *
Zen : then *
teasing : teething *   closing : clothing* *
seize : seethe *   breeze : breathe* *   rise : writhe* *

■

4 4 Phoneme Sequences

a nice thing * *it's thin* * *pass through* *	/sθ/
who's this? * *choose them* * *Jane's there* *	/zð/
the North Sea * *faiths* * *bath soap* *	/θs/
breathes * *with Zulus* * *mouths* *	/ðz/
it's nice though * *what's this?* * *chase them* *	/sð/
his thumb * *wise thoughts* * *as thunder* *	/zθ/
Bath Zoo * *death zone* * *both zebras* *	/θz/
the smooth side * *with certainty* *	/ðs/

■

4 2 2

'heðə, 'ʌðə, 'bɒðə
'fɜːðə, 'leðə, 'hiːðən
ðəʊ, ðæt, ðɪs
ðeə, ðiːz, ðaɪn
taɪð, ləʊð, briːð
leɪð, kləʊð, blaɪð

∎

4 3

sɪŋk : zɪŋk, suː : zuː, siːl : ziːl
'bʌsɪŋ : 'bʌzɪŋ, 'presədənt : 'prezədənt, 'fʌsɪ : 'fʌzɪ
siːs : siːz, daɪs : daɪz, praɪs : praɪz
θaɪ : ðaɪ
'iːθə : 'iːðə
riːθ : riːð, tiːθ : tiːð, maʊθ : maʊð
sʌm : θʌm, seɪn : θeɪn, sɔː : θɔː
mɪs : mɪθ, mɒs : mɒθ, fɔːs : fɔːθ
zen : ðen
'tiːzɪŋ : 'tiːðɪŋ, 'kləʊzɪŋ : 'kləʊðɪŋ
siːz : siːð, briːz : briːð, raɪz : raɪð

∎

4 4

ə 'naɪs 'θɪŋ, ɪts 'θɪn, 'pɑːs 'θruː
huːz 'ðɪs, 'tʃuːz ðəm, 'dʒeɪnz ðeə
ðə nɔːθ 'siː, feɪθs. 'bɑːθ 'səʊp
briːðz, wɪð 'zuːluːz, maʊðz
ɪts 'naɪs ðəʊ, wɒts 'ðɪs, 'tʃeɪs ðəm
hɪz 'θʌm, 'waɪz 'θɔːts, æz 'θʌndə
bɑːθ 'zuː, 'deθ ˌzəʊn, 'bəʊθ 'ziːbrəz
ðə 'smuːð 'saɪd, wɪð 'sɜːtntɪ

∎

39

4 5　Pronunciation of < -(e)s > {pl.}, {gen.}, {3.sg.pr.}

meets, takes, months *　　/s/　　/FC (except s, ʃ, tʃ)___
laughs, Pete's, Mike's *

bangs, lives, kegs, Ed's *　/z/　　/LC (except z, ʒ, dʒ)___
cows, buys, cities *　　　　　　/V___

kisses, loses, pushes *　　/ɪz/　　/s, z, ʃ, ʒ, tʃ, dʒ___
judge's, catches, barrages *

4 6　Singular /ɪs/, Plural /iːz/
basis : bases *　*crisis : crises* *　*analysis : analyses* *
■

4 7　Pronunciation of < x >
exercise, extra, exit *　　/ks/　　/ ~
axis, excite, exhibition *

exam, exact, example *　　/gz/　　/___'V
exist, anxiety, exhibit *　　　　　　(except < exc > 'V)
■

4 8　Some words with "silent s"
island, isle, Carlisle *
Grosvenor, aisle, corps *
Arkansas, Illinois, demesne *
■

4 9　Drill Sentences
　1　*This is the news.* *
　2　*This is the same as that.* *
　3　*Take it easy, brother.* *
　4　*Who's the author of "The Three Musketeers"?* *
　5　*His thoughts are on something else.* *
■
　6　*Martha chose those that were closest.* *
　7　*Susan always cleans the house on Thursdays.* *
　8　*What pleasant houses these are.* *
　9　*This seems to be the only thing Edith could think of.* *
　10　*These nouns seldom occur in the possessive case.* *
■

4 5

miːts, teɪks, mʌnθs
lɑːfs, piːts, maɪks
bæŋz, lɪvz, kegz, edz
kaʊz, baɪz, ˈsɪtɪz
ˈkɪsɪz, ˈluːzɪz, ˈpʊʃɪz
ˈdʒʌdʒɪz, ˈkætʃɪz, ˈbærɑːʒɪz

4 6

ˈbeɪsɪs : ˈbeɪsiːz, ˈkraɪsɪs : ˈkraɪsiːz, əˈnæləsɪs : əˈnæləsiːz
■

4 7

ˈeksəsaɪz, ˈekstrə, ˈeksɪt
ˈæksɪs, ɪkˈsaɪt, ˌeksɪˈbɪʃn
ɪɡˈzæm, ɪɡˈzækt, ɪɡˈzɑːmpl
ɪɡˈzɪst, æŋɡˈzaɪətɪ, ɪɡˈzɪbɪt
■

4 8

ˈaɪlənd, aɪl, kɑːˈlaɪl
ˈɡrəʊvnə, aɪl, kɔː
ˈɑːkənsɔː, ˌɪlɪˈnɔɪ, dɪˈmeɪn
■

4 9

1 ˈðɪs ɪz ðə ˈnjuːz.
2 ˈðɪs ɪz ðə ˈseɪm əz ˈðæt.
3 ˈteɪk ɪt ˈiːzɪ, ˈbrʌðə.
4 ˈhuːz ðɪ ˈɔːθər əv ðə ˈθriː mʌskəˈtɪəz.
5 hɪz ˈθɔːts ər ɒn ˈsʌmθɪŋ ˈels.
■

6 ˈmɑːθə tʃəuz ˈðəʊz ðət wə ˈkləʊsɪst.
7 ˈsuːzn ˈɔːlweɪz ˈkliːnz ðə ˈhaʊs ɒn ˈθɜːzdeɪz.
8 ˈwɒt ˈplezənt ˈhaʊzɪz ˈðiːz ˈɑː.
9 ˈðɪs ˈsiːmz tə biː ðɪ ˈəʊnlɪ ˈθɪŋ ˈiːdɪθ kʊd ˈθɪŋk ˈɒv.
10 ˈðiːz ˈnaʊnz ˈseldəm əˈkɜːr ɪn ðə pəˈzesɪv ˈkeɪs.
■

11 *Every youth knows the story of Robinson Crusoe.* *
12 *His expedition explored the northern parts of Missouri.* *
13 *Obviously, this month's rising gas prices are surprising.* *
14 *Swansea is an industrial city in South Wales.* *
■

15 *The city mouse lives in a house;*
The garden mouse lives in a bower,
He's friendly with the frogs and toads,
And sees the pretty plants in flower. *

The city mouse eats bread and cheese;
The garden mouse eats what he can;
We will not grudge him seeds and stocks,
Poor little timid furry man.
■   *Christina Georgina Rossetti* *

5   Fricatives /f, v/

5 1   Articulation Drills (Fortis)
Philip, fox, photograph, *
Aphrodite, hi-fi, draught *
trough, stuff, enough *

5 2   Major Allophone Drills (Lenis)

	Allophone	Context
loving, hover, heavy * *envy, ivy, divorce* *	fully v-d	/v___v
Vicky, very, vandal * *voodoo, vase, vex* *	part. dev-d	/#___
hive, move, leave * *serve, sieve, glove* *	dev-d	/___#

■

5 3   Minimal Pairs
fine : vine * *feel : veal* * *feud : viewed* * *fat : vat* *
rifle : rival * *define : divine* * *refuse : reviews* *
life : live * *proof : prove* * *fife : five* *
■

5 4   For Drill Sentences see 6.

11 ˈevrɪ ˈjuːθ ˈnəʊz ðə ˈstɔːrɪ əv ˈrɒbɪnsən ˈkruːsəʊ.
12 hɪz ekspɪˈdɪʃn ɪkˈsplɔːd ðə ˈnɔːðən ˈpɑːts əv mɪˈzʊərɪ.
13 ˈɒbvɪəslɪ, ˈðɪs ˈmʌnθs ˈraɪzɪŋ ˈgæs ˈpraɪsɪz ə səˈpraɪzɪŋ.
14 ˈswɒnzɪ ɪz ən ɪnˈdʌstrɪəl ˈsɪtɪ ɪn ˈsaʊθ ˈweɪlz.
■

15 ðə ˈsɪtɪ maʊs ˈlɪvz ɪn ə ˈhaʊs;
ðə ˈgɑːdn maʊs ˈlɪvz ɪn ə ˈbaʊə,
hiːz ˈfrendlɪ wɪð ðə ˈfrɒgz ən ˈtəʊdz,
ən ˈsiːz ðə ˈprɪtɪ ˈplɑːnts ɪn ˈflaʊə.

ðə ˈsɪtɪ maʊs iːts ˈbred ən ˈtʃiːz;
ðə ˈgɑːdn maʊs ˈiːts wɒt hɪ ˈkæn;
wɪ wɪl nɒt ˈgrʌdʒ hɪm ˈsiːdz ən ˈstɒks,
ˈpɔː lɪtl ˈtɪmɪd ˈfɜːrɪ ˈmæn.

■   krɪˈstiːnə dʒɔːˈdʒiːnə rɒˈsetɪ

5

5 1

ˈfɪlɪp, fɒks, ˈfəʊtəgrɑːf
ˌæfrəˈdaɪtɪ, ˈhaɪfaɪ, drɑːft
trɒf, stʌf, ɪˈnʌf

5 2

ˈlʌvɪŋ, ˈhɒvə, ˈhevɪ
envɪ, ˈaɪvɪ, dɪˈvɔːs
vɪkɪ, ˈverɪ, ˈvændl
ˈvuːduː, vɑːz, veks
haɪv, muːv, liːv
sɜːv, sɪv, glʌv
■

5 3

faɪn : vaɪn, fiːl : viːl, fjuːd : vjuːd, fæt : væt
ˈraɪfl : ˈraɪvl, dɪˈfaɪn : dɪˈvaɪn, rɪˈfjuːz : rɪˈvjuːz
laɪf : laɪv, pruːf : pruːv, faɪf : faɪv
■

6 Approximant /w/

6 1 Major Allophone Drills

	Allophone	Context
6 1 1 *we, Gwendolyn, inward* * *worm, wolf, bewitch* * *wigwam, Wycliffe, Wyoming* * *where, whistle, while* * ■	v-d	/ ~
6 1 2 *twist, twine, Twiggy* * *tweed, twig, Twain* * *quite, qualify, quack* * *quaint, queer, quiver* * ■	dev-d	/t___'V /k___'V (except sk)

6 1 3 Contrast:
Gwyn : *Quinn* * *guano* : *quote* *
dwell : *twelve* * *Dwight* : *twice* *
■

6 2 Minimal Pairs
wise : *vies* * *wet* : *vet* * *Wales* : *vales* *
worse : *verse* * *wick* : *Vic* * *wiper* : *viper* *
weird : *veered* * *wine* : *vine* * *wary* : *vary* *
■

6 3 Drill Sentences
1 *Walter wanted vodka and wine.* *
2 *His advice was too obvious.* *
3 *Winifred read Advanced Linguistics.* *
4 *Whether the weather be fine*
   Or whether the weather be not,
   Whether the weather be cold
   Or whether the weather be hot,
   We'll weather the weather
   Whatever the weather,
   Whether we like it or not. *

■

6

6 1

6 1 1
wiː, ˈgwendəlɪn, ˈɪnwəd
wɜːm, wʊlf, brˈwɪtʃ
ˈwɪgwæm, ˈwɪklɪf, waɪˈəʊmɪŋ
weə, ˈwɪsl, waɪl

∎

6 1 2
twɪst, twaɪn, ˈtwɪgɪ
twiːd, twɪg, tweɪn
kwaɪt, ˈkwɒlɪfaɪ, kwæk
kweɪnt, kwɪə, ˈkwɪvə

∎

6 1 3
gwɪn : kwɪn,   ˈgwɑːnəʊ : kwəʊt
dwel : twelv,   dwaɪt : twaɪs

∎

6 2
waɪz : vaɪz,   wet : vet,   weɪlz : veɪlz
wɜːs : vɜːs,   wɪk : vɪk,   ˈwaɪpə : ˈvaɪpə
wɪəd : vɪəd,   waɪn : vaɪn,   ˈweərɪ : ˈveərɪ

∎

6 3

1 ˈwɔːltə ˈwɒntɪd ˈvɒdkər ənd ˈwaɪn.
2 hɪz ədˈvaɪs wəz ˈtuː ˈɒbvɪəs.
3 ˈwɪnɪfred red ədˈvɑːnst lɪŋˈgwɪstɪks.
4 ˈweðə ðə ˈweðə bɪ ˈfaɪn
  ɔː ˈweðə ðə ˈweðə bɪ ˈnɒt,
  ˈweðə ðə ˈweðə bɪ ˈkəʊld
  ɔː ˈweðə ðə ˈweðə bɪ ˈhɒt
  wiːl ˈweðə ðə ˈweðə
  wɒtˈevə ðə ˈweðə,
  ˈweðə wɪ ˈlaɪk ɪt ɔː ˈnɒt.

∎

5   *We were invited for a glass of whiskey.* *
6   *The Wizard of Oz is a wonderful movie.* *
7   *We value the love of our brothers and sisters.* *
8   *Is it worth while working in the vineyard?* *
9   *Vampires usually ravish virgins.* *

■

10 *What weather will Vivian have in Venice?* *
11 *We watched the Woodstock Festival on television.* *
12 *She couldn't find any vegetables at Woolworth's.* *
13 *They visited Worcester and Wolverhampton.* *
14 *Harvard University and the University of Pennsylvania are very well known.* *

■

15 *The question is whether Wayne will wait.* *
16 *Whatever would Vera do without her microwave oven?* *
17 *What a witty conversation that was.* *
18 *Which is the wicked witch that wished the wicked wish?* *
19 *A cowboy's work is never done.* *

■

20 *There was an old woman, and what do you think?*
    She lived upon nothing but victuals and drink; *

    And though victuals and drink were the chief of her diet,
    This plaguy old woman could never be quiet. *

    She went to the baker, to buy her some bread,
    And when she came home, her old husband was dead; *

    She went to the clerk to toll the bell,
    And when she came home, her old husband was well. *

■

5   wi wər inˈvaitid fər ə ˈglɑːs əv ˈwiski.
6   ðə ˈwizəd əv ˈɒz iz ə ˈwʌndəful ˈmuːvi.
7   wi ˈvælju: ðə ˈlʌv əv ɑːˈbrʌðəz ən ˈsistəz.
8   iz it ˈwɜːθ ˈwail ˈwɜːkiŋ in ðə ˈvinjəd?
9   ˈvæmpaiəz ˈjuːʒəli ˈræviʃ ˈvɜːdʒinz.

■

10 ˈwɒt ˈweðə wil ˈvivjən ˈhæv in ˈvenis?
11 wi ˈwɒtʃt ðə ˈwudstɒk ˈfestivl ɒn ˈteləviʒn.
12 ʃi ˈkudnt ˈfaind eni ˈvedʒtəblz ət ˈwulwəθs.
13 ðei ˈvizitid ˈwustər ənd ˈwulvəhæmtən.
14 ˈhɑːvəd juːniˈvɜːsiti ənd ðə juːniˈvɜːsiti əv pensilˈveinjər ə ˈveri ˈwel ˈnəun.

■

15 ðə ˈkwestʃn ˈiz weðə ˈwein wil ˈweit.
16 wɒtˈevə wud ˈviərə ˈduː wiðˈaut hə ˈmaikrəuweiv ˈʌvn?
17 ˈwɒt ə ˈwiti kɒnvəˈseiʃn ðæt ˈwɒz.
18 ˈwitʃ iz ðə ˈwikid ˈwitʃ ðət ˈwiʃt ðə ˈwikid ˈwiʃ?
19 ə ˈkauboiz ˈwɜːk iz ˈnevə ˈdʌn.

■

20 ðeə ˈwɒz ən əuld ˈwumən, ənd ˈwɒt du ju ˈθiŋk?
    ʃi ˈlivd əpɒn ˈnʌθiŋ bət ˈvitlz ən ˈdriŋk;
    ənd ðəu ˈvitlz ən ˈdriŋk wə ðə ˈtʃiːf əv hə ˈdaiət,
    ðis ˈpleigi əuld ˈwumən kud ˈnevə bi ˈkwaiət.
    ʃi ˈwent tə ðə ˈbeikə, tə ˈbai hə səm ˈbred,
    ənd ˈwen ʃi keim ˈhəum, hər əuld ˈhʌzbənd wəz ˈded;
    ʃi ˈwent tə ðə ˈklɑːk tə ˈtəul ðə ˈbel,
    ənd ˈwen ʃi keim ˈhəum, hər əuld ˈhʌzbənd wəz ˈwel.

■

7 Approximant /j/

7 1 Major Allophone Drills

		Allophone	Context
7 1 1	*yard, yoghourt, yesterday* * *stew, butane, beyond* * *university,* **Buick,** *altitude* *	v-d	/ ~
7 1 2	*puma, pure, pupil* * Teuton, tunic, Tudor* * *cure, queue, accuse* * ■	dev-d	/p, t, k____'V (except sp, st, sk)

7 1 3 Contrast:

pews : Bews *   *pewter : beauty* *   *puke : bugle* *
Tuke : duke *   *tune : dune* *   *tutor : duty* *
Gue : Kew *   *ague : forsake you* *
■

7 2 Drill Sentences

1 *Yesterday they played new music on the radio.* *
2 *Could you pursue the matter further?* *
3 *What a nuisance!* *
4 *This news is ridiculous.* *
5 *Our yield of onions was superb.* *
■

6 *Does Yolanda eat cucumbers?* *
7 *She knew where to queue up for the tube.* *
8 *Mr Young flew from the Grand Canyon to New York.* *
9 *They argued about the use of nuclear fuel.* *
10 *Dr Yardley's cure for tuberculosis and pneumonia was spectacular.* *

■

7

7 1

7 1 1
jɑːd, ˈjɒŋɡət, ˈjestədeɪ
stjuː, ˈbjuːteɪn, bɪˈjɒnd
juːnɪˈvɜːsətɪ, ˈbjuːɪk, ˈæltɪtjuːd

7 1 2
ˈpjuːmə, pjʊə, ˈpjuːpl
ˈtjuːtən, ˈtjuːnɪk, ˈtjuːdə
kjʊə, kjuː, əˈkjuːz

∎

7 1 3
pjuːz : bjuːz, ˈpjuːtə : ˈbjuːtɪ, pjuːk : ˈbjuːɡl
tjuːk : djuːk, tjuːn : djuːn, ˈtjuːtə : ˈdjuːtɪ
ɡjuː : kjuː, ˈeɪɡjuː : fɔːˈseɪk juː

∎

7 2

1 ˈjestədeɪ ðeɪ ˈpleɪd ˈnjuː ˈmjuːzɪk ɒn ðə ˈreɪdɪəʊ.
2 ˈkʊd jʊ pəˈsjuː ðə ˈmætə ˈfɜːðə?
3 ˈwɒt ə ˈnjuːsns!
4 ˈðɪs ˈnjuːz ɪz rɪˈdɪkjʊləs.
5 ɑː ˈjiːld əv ˈʌnjənz wəz sʊˈpɜːb.

∎

6 ˈdʌz jɒˈlændər ˈiːt ˈkjuːkʌmbəz?
7 ʃɪ ˈnjuː ˈweə tə ˈkjuː ˈʌp fə ðə ˈtjuːb.
8 ˈmɪstə ˈjʌŋ ˈfluː frəm ðə ˈɡrænd ˈkænjən tə ˈnjuː ˈjɔːk.
9 ðeɪ ˈɑːɡjuːd əbaʊt ðə ˈjuːs əv ˈnjuːklɪə ˈfjʊəl.
10 dɒktə ˈjɑːdlɪz ˈkjʊə fə tjuːbɜːkjʊˈləʊsɪs ənd njuːˈməʊnjə wəz spekˈtækjʊlə.

∎

8 Lateral /l/

8 1 Major Allophone Drills

	Allophone	Context
8 1 1 *land, lord, leak* *	clear /l/	/___V
hallelujah, sleep, jelly *		
kullo, flee, filling *		
sell out, pull up, fill it *		
all of it, fall off, I'll ask *		
lure, lieu, stallion *		/___j
billion, will you, failure *		
■		

8 1 2 *silk, self, old* *	dark /l/	/___C
quilt, hills, pulp *		
filth, pulse, mulch *		
hell, fill, sell *		/___#
all, pull, while *		(except
middle, table, apple *		___#V, j)
cool, roll, fool *		
■		

8 1 3 *loud, Pole, will* *	v-d	/~
silly, milk, million *		
gland, blow, idle *		
please, plough, place *	dev-d	/p, k___'V
clover, cleave, clash *		(except sp, sk)
■		

8 1 4 Contrast:

class : *glass* * *clean* : *glean* * *clad* : *glad* *
close : *glows* * *clue* : *glue* * *Clyde* : *glide* *
plead : *bleed* * *plush* : *blush* * *plot* : *blot* *
pleat : *bleat* * *plank* : *blank* * *plays* : *blaze* *
■

8

8 1

8 1 1
lænd, lɔːd, liːk
ˌhæləˈluːjə, sliːp, ˈdʒelɪ
həˈləʊ, fliː, ˈfɪlɪŋ
sel ˈaʊt, pʊl ˈʌp, ˈfɪl ɪt
ˈɔːl əv ɪt, fɔːl ɒf, aɪl ˈɑːsk
ljʊə, ljuː, ˈstæljən
ˈbɪljən, ˈwɪl jʊ, ˈfeɪljə
∎

8 1 2
sɪlk, self, əʊld
kwɪlt, hɪlz, pʌlp
fɪlθ, pʌls, mʌltʃ
hel, fɪl, sel
ɔːl, pʊl, waɪl
ˈmɪdl, ˈteɪbl, ˈæpl
kuːl, rəʊl, fuːl
∎

8 1 3
laʊd, pəʊl, wɪl
ˈsɪlɪ, mɪlk, ˈmɪljən
glænd, bləʊ, ˈaɪdl
pliːz, plaʊ, pleɪs
ˈkləʊvə, kliːv, klæʃ
∎

8 1 4
klɑːs : glɑːs, kliːn : gliːn, klæd : glæd
kləʊz : gləʊz, kluː : gluː, klaɪd : glaɪd
pliːd : bliːd, plʌʃ : blʌʃ, plɒt : blɒt
pliːt : bliːt, plæŋk : blæŋk, pleɪz : bleɪz
∎

8 2 Some words with "silent l"
salmon, psalm, alms *
folk, colonel, halfpenny *
balm, half, salve *

■

8 3 Syllabic /l/
pedal, battle, whistle *
Ethel, devil, kennel *

■

8 4 Drill Sentences

1 *All you need is love.* *
2 *He's a jolly good fellow.* *
3 *We all live in a yellow submarine.* *
4 *What a terrible personality conflict.* *

■

5 Listen to the following passage in its entirety. Then drill each sentence separately.

Dear Lucy,
You will probably be a little surprised to get this
letter. * *If you recall, we met at your Uncle William's*
last July during my holiday in London. * *I have since*
finished reading law at Keele, and am now living in a
small flat near the Elephant and Castle. * *Earlier*
this year, in April actually, I applied to Lloyd's
of London for a position and was lucky enough to be selected. *
My responsibilities include the handling of small claims. *
Although I find my job challenging, life
here tends to be a little dull for an old bachelor like
myself. * *To make a long story short, would you allow*
me to invite you to a play or a film one evening next week? *
The 'Aldwich', for example, will still be playing "All's
well that ends well", while the 'Royal' is showing
the musical "My Fair Lady". * *Please let me know as soon*
as possible whether you will be able to come. * *I would be*
extremely pleased to see you again. *
Looking forward to your reply,

　　　　　　　　　　　　　Yours sincerely,
■　　　　　　　　　　　　*Malcolm Lowell.* *

8 2

ˈsæmən, sɑːm, ɑːmz
fəʊk, ˈkɜːnl, ˈheɪpənɪ
bɑːm, hɑːf, sɑːv
∎

8 3

ˈpedl, ˈbætl, ˈwɪsl
ˈeθl, ˈdevl, ˈkenl
∎

8 4

1 ˈɔːl jʊ ˈniːd ɪz ˈlʌv.
2 hiːz ə ˈdʒɒlɪ ɡʊd ˈfeləʊ.
3 wɪ ˈɔːl ˈlɪv ɪn ə ˈjeləʊ sʌbməˈriːn.
4 wɒt ə ˈterɪbl pɜːsəˈnælətɪ ˈkɒnflɪkt.
∎

5

ˈdɪə ˈluːsɪ,
jʊ wɪl ˈprɒbəblɪ bɪ ə ˈlɪtl səˈpraɪzd tə ˈget ðɪs
ˈletə. ɪf jʊ rɪˈkɔːl, wɪ ˈmet ət jɔːr ʌŋkl ˈwɪljəmz
ˈlɑːs dʒuːˈlaɪ ˈdjʊərɪŋ maɪ ˈhɒlɪdeɪ ɪn ˈlʌndən. aɪv ˈsɪns
ˈfɪnɪʃt ˈriːdɪŋ ˈlɔː ət ˈkiːl, ənd əm ˈnaʊ ˈlɪvɪŋ ɪn ə
ˈsmɔːl ˈflæt nɪə ðɪ ˈeləfənt ən ˈkɑːsl. ˈɜːlɪə
ðɪs ˈjɪə, ɪn ˈeɪprəl ˈæktʃəlɪ, aɪ əˈplaɪd tə ˈlɔɪdz
əv ˈlʌndən fər ə pəˈzɪʃn ənd wəz ˈlʌkɪ ɪˈnʌf tə bɪ sɪˈlektɪd.
maɪ rɪspɒnsɪˈbɪlɪtɪz ɪŋˈkluːd ðə ˈhændlɪŋ əv ˈsmɔːl ˈkleɪmz.
ɔːlˈðəʊ aɪ faɪnd maɪ ˈdʒɒb ˈtʃæləndʒɪŋ, ˈlaɪf
hɪə ˈtendz tə bɪ ə lɪtl ˈdʌl fər ən ˈəʊld ˈbætʃələ ˈlaɪk
maɪˈself. tə meɪk ə lɒŋ ˈstɔːrɪ ˈʃɔːt, ˈwʊd jʊ əˈlaʊ
mɪ tʊ ɪnˈvaɪt jʊ tʊ əˈpleɪ ɔːr ə ˈfɪlm ˈwʌn ˈiːvnɪŋ ˈneks ˈwiːk?
ðɪ ˈɔːldwɪtʃ, fər ɪɡˈzɑːmpl, wɪl ˈstɪl bɪ ˈpleɪɪŋ ˈɔːlz
ˈwel ðət endz wel, waɪl ðə rɔɪəl ɪz ʃəʊɪŋ
ðə ˈmjuːzɪkl ˈmaɪ feə ˈleɪdɪ. pliːz let mɪ ˈnəʊ əz ˈsuːn
əz ˈpɒsɪbl ˈweðə jʊ wəl bɪ ˈeɪbl tə ˈkʌm. aɪ wəd bɪ
ɪkˈstriːmlɪ pliːzd tə siː juː əˈgen.
ˈlʊkɪŋ ˈfɔːwəd tə jɔː rɪˈplaɪ,

∎
                        ˈjɔːz sɪnˈsɪəlɪ,
                        ˈmælkəm ˈləʊəl.

9 Fricatives /ʃ, ʒ/

9 1 Articulation Drills (Fortis)
hush, bush, dish *
geisha, fissure, luxury *
shabby, schedule, shawl *

9 2 Major Allophone Drills (Lenis)

	Allophone	Context
measure, adhesion, leisure *	fully v-d	/v___v
seizure, usual, treasure *		
genre, gigolo, gigue *	part. dev-d	/#___
beige, camouflage, prestige *	dev-d	/___#

∎

9 3 Contrast:
pleasure : *pressure* *   *rouge* : *ruche* *   *vision* : *mission* *
azure : *Asher* *   *occasion* : *relation* *
∎

9 4 For Drill Sentences see 10.

10 Affricates /tʃ, dʒ/

10 1 Articulation Drills (Fortis)
China, cheque, chair *
actual, archbishop, bachelor *
pitch, bleach, watch *

10 2 Major Allophone Drills (Lenis)

	Allophone	Context
Kojak, magic, adjunct *	fully v-d	/v___v
aging, adjourn, suggest *		
Jimmy, jungle, join *	part dev-d	/#___
Jesus, German, giant *		
badge, lodge, luggage *	dev-d	/___#
garage, wedge, huge *		

∎

9

9 1

hʌʃ, bʊʃ, dɪʃ
ˈgeɪʃə, ˈfɪʃə, ˈlʌkʃərɪ
ˈʃæbɪ, ˈʃedjuːl, ʃɔːl

9 2

ˈmeʒə, ədˈhiːʒn, ˈleʒə
ˈsiːʒə, ˈjuːʒwəl, ˈtreʒə
ˈʒɑːnrə, ˈʒɪgələʊ, ʒiːg
beɪʒ, ˈkæmʊflɑːʒ, preˈstiːʒ
■

9 3

ˈpleʒə : ˈpreʃə,   ruːʒ : ruːʃ,   ˈvɪʒn : ˈmɪʃn
ˈæʒə : ˈæʃə,   əˈkeɪʒn : rɪˈleɪʃn
■

10

10 1

ˈtʃaɪnə, tʃek, tʃeə
ˈæktʃʊəl, ˌɑːtʃˈbɪʃəp, ˈbætʃələ
pɪtʃ, bliːtʃ, wɒtʃ

10 2

ˈkəʊdʒæk, ˈmædʒɪk, ˈædʒʌŋkt
ˈeɪdʒɪŋ, əˈdʒɜːn, səˈdʒest
ˈdʒɪmɪ, ˈdʒʌŋgl, dʒɔɪn
ˈdʒiːzəs, ˈdʒɜːmən, ˈdʒaɪənt
bædʒ, lɒdʒ, ˈlʌgɪdʒ
ˈgærɑːdʒ, wedʒ, hjuːdʒ
■

10 3 Minimal Pairs

choke : joke * chest : jest * choose : Jews *
beseeching : besieging * etching : edging *
larch : large * aitch : age * lunch : lunge *
shoe : chew : Jew * shin : chin : gin * sherry : cherry : Jerry *
leisure : ledger : lecher * Pershing : purging : perching *
cash : cadge : catch * bash : badge : batch *

■

10 4 Pronunciation of <-tion>

fiction, invention, protection *	/ʃn/	/ ~
caption, exception, abortion *		
question, suggestion, digestion *	/tʃn/	/s___
combustion, congestion *		

■

10 5 Drill Sentences

1 *Mr. Jones was a lecherous old codger. **
2 *This machine is exceptionally functional. **
3 *We actually appreciated the change. **
4 *The children were drinking orange juice. **
5 *She purchased some genuine Limoges china. **

■

6 *Her decision to accept the challenge was unusual. **
7 *Jean had the pleasure of meeting a gentleman from Greenwich. **
8 *They chose a jumbo jet for their journey. **
9 *The hijacker was captured in Djibouti. **
10 *The Japanese judo team visited Germany. **

■

11 *Pidgin English is a traditional trade language on the Fiji Islands. **
12 *Energy conservation is a controversial subject. **
13 *Two Germans were gaoled in Czechoslovakia on trumped-up charges of espionage. **
14 *The persecution of Jews in the Middle Ages was essentially a question of religious superstition. **
15 *Ginger Rogers was a charming individual. **

■

10 3

tʃəʊk : dʒəʊk, tʃest : dʒest, tʃuːz : dʒuːz
brˈsiːtʃɪŋ : brˈsiːdʒɪŋ, ˈetʃɪŋ : ˈedʒɪŋ
lɑːtʃ : lɑːdʒ, eɪtʃ : eɪdʒ, lʌntʃ : lʌndʒ
ʃuː : tʃuː : dʒuː, ʃɪn : tʃɪn : dʒɪn, ˈʃerɪ : ˈtʃerɪ : ˈdʒerɪ
ˈleʒə : ˈledʒə : ˈletʃə, ˈpɜːʃɪŋ : ˈpɜːdʒɪŋ : ˈpɜːtʃɪŋ
kæʃ : kædʒ : kætʃ, bæʃ : bædʒ : bætʃ

∎

10 4

ˈfɪkʃn, ɪnˈvenʃn, prəˈtekʃn
ˈkæpʃn, ɪkˈsepʃn, əˈbɔːʃn
ˈkwestʃn, səˈdʒestʃn, daɪˈdʒestʃn
kəm bʌstʃn, kən dʒestʃn

∎

10 5

1 mɪstə ˈdʒəʊnz wəz ə ˈletʃrəs ˈəʊld ˈkɒdʒə.
2 ˈðɪs məˈʃiːn ɪz ɪkˈsepʃnəlɪ ˈfʌŋkʃnl.
3 wɪ ˈæktʃəlɪ əˈpriːʃʃeɪtɪd ðə ˈtʃeɪndʒ.
4 ðə ˈtʃɪldrən wə ˈdrɪŋkɪŋ ˈɒrɪndʒ ˈdʒuːs.
5 ʃɪ ˈpɜːtʃəst səm ˈdʒenjʊɪn lɪˈməʊʒ ˈtʃaɪnə.

∎

6 hə dɪˈsɪʒn tʊ əkˈsept ðə ˈtʃæləndʒ wəz ʌnˈjuːʒwəl.
7 ˈdʒiːn hæd ðə ˈpleʒər əv ˈmiːtɪŋ ə ˈdʒentlmən frəm ˈgrɪnɪdʒ.
8 ðeɪ ˈtʃəʊz ə ˈdʒʌmbəʊ ˈdʒet fə ðeə ˈdʒɜːnɪ.
9 ðə ˈhaɪdʒækə wəz ˈkæptʃəd ɪn dʒɪˈbuːtɪ.
10 ðə ˈdʒæpəniːz ˈdʒuːdəʊ ˈtiːm ˈvɪzɪtɪd ˈdʒɜːməni.

∎

11 ˈpɪdʒɪn ˈɪŋglɪʃ ɪz ə trəˈdɪʃnl treɪd ˈlæŋgwɪdʒ ɒn ðə ˈfiːdʒiː ˈaɪləndz.
12 ˈenədʒɪ kɒnsəˈveɪʃn ɪz ə kɒntrəˈvɜːʃl ˈsʌbdʒekt.
13 ˈtuː ˈdʒɜːmənz wə ˈdʒeɪld ɪn tʃekəsləˈvɑːkjər ɒn ˈtrʌmpt ʌp ˈtʃɑːdʒɪz əv ˈespjənɑːʒ.
14 ðə pɜːsəˈkjuːʃn əv ˈdʒuːz ɪn ðə ˈmɪdl ˈeɪdʒɪz wəz ɪˈsenʃlɪ ə ˈkwestʃn əv rɪˈlɪdʒəs sjuːpəˈstɪʃn.
15 ˈdʒɪndʒə ˈrɒdʒəz wəz ə ˈtʃɑːmɪŋ ɪndɪˈvɪdʒʊəl.

∎

16 *Charlotte was anxious to drive from Chicago to Jackson, Michigan.* *
17 *George came to the conclusion that French champagne can be dangerous.* *
18 *Might I suggest that this budget meeting be adjourned.* *
19 *The judge charged him with juvenile delinquency.* *
20 *Jack be nimble, Jack be quick,*
   Jack jump over the candlestick. *
∎

11 Fricative /h/

11 1 Articulation Drills
hero, hurt, who, whore *
heretic, hazard, history *
Navajo, Mojave, Heidelberg *

11 2 Contrast:
heat : eat * *hill : ill* * *hat : at* *
harrow : arrow * *heart : art* * *hold : old* *

11 3 Some words with "silent h"
shepherd, prohibition, vehicle *
hour, honour, heir, honest *
forehead, Birmingham, Durham *
∎

11 4 For Drill Sentences see 12.

12 Nasal /m, n, ŋ /

12 1 Articulation Drills
mass, mock, autumn *
poem, tumor, Amy *
nill, gnaw, mnemonic *
annoyed, barn, done *
cooking, among, lung *
harangue, ringing, pangs *
∎

16 ˈʃɑːlət wəz ˈæŋkʃəs tə ˈdraɪv frəm ʃɪˈkɑːgəʊ tə ˈdʒæksn̩, ˈmɪʃɪgən.

17 ˈdʒɔːdʒ keɪm tə ðə kənˈkluːʒn̩ ðət ˈfrenʃ ʃæmˈpeɪn kən bɪ ˈdeɪndʒərəs.

18 ˈmaɪt aɪ səˈdʒest ðət ˈðɪs ˈbʌdʒɪt miːtɪŋ bɪ əˈdʒɜːnd.

19 ðə ˈdʒʌdʒ ˈtʃɑːdʒd hɪm wɪð ˈdʒuːvənaɪl dɪˈlɪŋkwənsɪ.

20 ˈdʒæk bɪ ˈnɪmbl̩, ˈdʒæk bɪ ˈkwɪk,
ˈdʒæk dʒʌmp ˈəʊvə ðə ˈkændl̩ˈstɪk.

∎

11

11 1

ˈhɪərəʊ, hɜːt, huː, hɔː
ˈherətɪk, ˈhæzəd, ˈhɪstrɪ
ˈnævəhəʊ, məˈhɑːvɪ, ˈhaɪdlbɜːg

11 2

hiːt : iːt, hɪl : ɪl, hæt : æt
ˈhærəʊ : ˈærəʊ, hɑːt : ɑːt, həʊld : əʊld

11 3

ˈʃepəd, ˌprəʊɪˈbɪʃn, ˈviːɪkl
ˈaʊə, ˈɒnə, eə, ˈɒnɪst
ˈfɒrɪd, ˈbɜːmɪŋəm, ˈdʌrəm

∎

12

12 1

mæs, mɒk, ˈɔːtəm
ˈpəʊəm, ˈtjuːmə, ˈeɪmɪ
nɪl, nɔː, niːˈmɒnɪk
əˈnɔɪd, bɑːn, dʌn
ˈkʊkɪŋ, əˈmʌŋ, lʌŋ
həˈræŋ, ˈrɪŋɪŋ, pæŋz

∎

12 2 /ŋ:ŋg:ŋk:gn/

sing, singer *	/ŋ/
wrong, wronging *	
bang, banging *	
long, young, strong *	
longer, longest *	/ŋg/
younger, youngest *	
stronger, strongest *	
finger, anger, angry *	/ŋg/
hunger, hungry, bingo *	
English, bungalow, single *	
anchor, uncle, Lancashire *	/ŋk/
ink, twinkle, hanky-panky *	
malignant, incognito, ignorant *	/gn/
magnet, ignite, agnostic *	

■

12 3 Contrast:

wind : winged * *band : banged* * *sun : sung* *
kin : king * *tan : tang* * *Hanover : hang-over* *
rang : rank * *sing : sink* * *bang : bank* *
cling : clink * *Ming : mink* * *hanger : hanker* *

■

12 4 /ən/ or Syllabic /n/?

person, given, pollen *	/(ə)n/	/ ~
oxen, ordinary, explanation *		
eleven, orphan, nation *		
cotton, hidden, sudden *	/n/	/t, d___
German, mountain, Washington *	/ən/	/nas.___
Arlington, London, Lincoln *		/nas.+plos.___
common, lemon, cannon *		

■

12 2

sɪŋ, ˈsɪŋə
rɒŋ, ˈrɒŋɪŋ
bæŋ, ˈbæŋɪŋ
lɒŋ, jʌŋ, strɒŋ
ˈlɒŋgə, ˈlɒŋgɪst
ˈjʌŋgə, ˈjʌŋgɪst
ˈstrɒŋgə, ˈstrɒŋgɪst
ˈfɪŋgə, ˈæŋgə, ˈæŋgrɪ
ˈhʌŋgə, ˈhʌŋgrɪ, ˈbɪŋgəʊ
ˈɪŋglɪʃ, ˈbʌŋgələʊ, ˈsɪŋgl
ˈæŋkə, ˈʌŋkl, ˈlæŋkəʃə
ɪŋk, ˈtwɪŋkl, ˈhæŋkɪˈpæŋkɪ
məˈlɪgnənt, ˌɪnkɒgˈniːtəʊ, ˈɪgnərənt
ˈmægnɪt, ɪgˈnaɪt, əgˈnɒstɪk

■

12 3

wɪnd : wɪŋd, bænd : bæŋd, sʌn : sʌŋ
kɪn : kɪŋ, tæn : tæŋ, ˈhænəʊvə : ˈhæŋəʊvə
ræn : ræŋk, sɪŋ : sɪŋk, bæn : bæŋk
klɪŋ : klɪŋk, mɪŋ : mɪŋk, ˈhæŋə : ˈhæŋkə

■

12 4

ˈpɜːsn, ˈgɪvn, ˈpɒlən
ˈɒksn, ˈɔːdnrɪ, ˌekspləˈneɪʃn
ˈlevn, ˈɔːfn, ˈneɪʃn
ˈkɒtn, ˈhɪdn, ˈsʌdn
ˈdʒɜːmən, ˈmaʊntən, ˈwɒʃɪŋtən
ˈɑːlɪŋtən, ˈlʌndən, ˈlɪŋkən
ˈkɒmən, ˈlemən, ˈkænən

■

12 5 Drill Sentences

1. *In Hertford, Hereford and Hampshire hurricanes hardly ever happen.* *
2. *Honestly, the whole thing was utterly ridiculous.* *
3. *Who wouldn't have heard of Homer?* *
4. *The heroine had hundreds of honourable suitors.* *
5. *His company sent him on a tour to Brighton, London, Lincoln and Durham.* *

■

6. *I can't remember a single thing.* *
7. *Henry and Hilary went to Hungary on their honeymoon.* *
8. *He came home, hungry as a hunter.* *
9. *Robin Hood lived in the surroundings of Nottingham.* *
10. *It would be wrong to think that Bangor is in England.* *

■

13 Front Vowel /i:/

13 1 Major Allophone Drills

		Allophone	Context
13 1 1	*beech, relief, critique* * *sheet, peep, grease* *	short.	/___FC[1]
13 1 2	*intrigue, feeds, cream* * *routine, receive, wield* *	length.	/___LC[1]
13 1 3	*plea, degree, trustee* * *quay, bourgeoisie, bee* *	diphth.	/___#

■

13 1 4 Contrast:

fleece : fleas *   *piece : peas* *   *meat : meed* *   *heat : heed* *
neat : knead *   *leaf : leave* *   *belief : believe* *   *cease : seize* *

■

13 2 For Drill Sentences see 14.

---

[1] A more detailed and exact rule for the distribution of shortened and lengthened stressed vowel allophones here and below would read:
/___(nas., lat.) FC (<-ed>, <-(e)s>)# and
/___(nas., lat.) LC (<-ed>, <-(e)s>)#.

12 5

1. ɪn ˈhɑːtʃəd, ˈherəfəd ənd ˈhæmpʃə ˈhʌrɪkənz ˈhɑːdlɪ ˈevə ˈhæpn.
2. ˈɒnɪstlɪ, ðə ˈhəʊl ˈθɪŋ wəz ˈʌtəlɪ rɪˈdɪkjʊləs.
3. ˈhuː ˈwʊdnt əv ˈhɜːd əv ˈhəʊmə?
4. ðə ˈherəʊɪn hæd ˈhʌndrədz əv ˈɒnərəbl ˈsuːtəz.
5. hɪz ˈkʌmpənɪ ˈsent ɪm ɒn ə ˈtʊə tə ˈbraɪtn, ˈlʌndən, ˈlɪŋkən ən ˈdʌrəm.

∎

6. aɪ ˈkɑːnt rɪˈmembər ə ˈsɪŋgl ˈθɪŋ.
7. ˈhenrɪ ənd ˈhɪlərɪ went tə ˈhʌŋgərɪ ɒn ðeə ˈhʌnɪmuːn.
8. hɪ keɪm ˈhəʊm, ˈhʌŋgrɪ əz ə ˈhʌntə.
9. ˈrɒbɪn ˈhʊd ˈlɪvd ɪn ðə səˈraʊndɪŋz əv ˈnɒtɪŋəm.
10. ɪt wʊd bɪ ˈrɒŋ tə ˈθɪŋk ðət ˈbæŋgər ɪz ɪn ˈɪŋglənd.

∎

13

13 1

biːtʃ, rɪˈliːf, krɪˈtiːk
ʃiːt, piːp, griːs
ɪnˈtriːg, fiːdz, kriːm
ruːtiːn, rɪˈsiːv, wiːld
pliː, dɪˈgriː, ˌtrʌsˈtiː
kiː, ˌbʊəʒwɑːˈziː, biː

∎

fliːs : fliːz, piːs : piːz, miːt : miːd, hiːt : hiːd
niːt : niːd, liːf : liːv, bəˈliːf : bəˈliːv, siːs : siːz

∎

14 Front-Central Vowel /ɪ/

14 1 Major Allophone Drills

		Allophone	Context
14 1 1	*ditch, stiff, mischief* * *abyss, this, fix* *	short.	/___FC
14 1 2	*give, gin, hymn* * *sieve, bridge, fig* *	length.	/___LC
14 1 3	*city, university, busy* * *silly, specialty, pity* *	short.	/.___#

■

14 1 4 Contrast:
bit : bid * *wick : wig* * *bricks : Briggs* *
nip : nib * *hiss : his* * *vis : viz.* *
■

14 2 /ɪ/ not /j/!
pronunciation * *mediocre* * *superior* *
inferior * *partiality* * *speciality* *
negotiation * *denunciation* * *familiarity* *
■

14 3 Minimal Pairs
lick : leak * *wit : wheat* * *lip : leap* * *hid : heed* *
hill : heal * *fill : feel* * *fizz : fees* * *nill : Neill* *
sit : Cid * *seat : seed* * *sit : Cid : seat : seed* *
lit : lid * *leet : lead* * *lit : lid : leet : lead* *
■

14 4 Drill Sentences
1 *Give me the key, please.* *
2 *These people are terribly conceited.* *
3 *I before E except after C.*
4 *They were guaranteed three weeks' salary.* *
5 *Immigration into Britain is strictly regulated.* *

■

14

14 1

dɪtʃ, stɪf, ˈmɪstʃɪf
əˈbɪs, ðɪs, fɪks
gɪv, dʒɪn, hɪm
sɪv, brɪdʒ, fɪg
ˈsɪtɪ, juːnɪˈvɜːsɪtɪ, ˈbɪzɪ
ˈsɪlɪ, ˈspeʃltɪ, ˈpɪtɪ
∎

bɪt : bɪd, wɪk : wɪg, brɪks : brɪgz
nɪp : nɪb, hɪs : hɪz, vɪs : vɪz
∎

14 2

prəˌnʌnsɪˈeɪʃn, ˌmiːdɪˈəʊkə, suːˈpɪərɪə
ɪnˈfɪərɪə, ˌpɑːʃɪˈælətɪ, ˌspeʃɪˈælətɪ
nəˌgəʊsɪˈeɪʃn, dɪˌnʌnsɪˈeɪʃn, fəˌmɪlɪˈærətɪ
∎

14 3

lɪk : liːk, wɪt : wiːt, lɪp : liːp, hɪd : hiːd
hɪl : hiːl, fɪl : fiːl, fɪz : fiːz, nɪl : niːl
sɪt : sɪd, siːt : siːd, sɪt : sɪd : siːt : siːd
lɪt : lɪd, liːt : liːd, lɪt : lɪd : liːt : liːd
∎

14 4

1 ˈgɪv mɪ ðə ˈkiː ˈpliːz.
2 ˈðiːz ˈpiːpl ə ˈterəblɪ kənˈsiːtɪd.
3 ˈaɪ bəfɔːr ˈiː ɪkˈsept ɑːftə ˈsiː.
4 ðeɪ wə ˈgærəntiːd ˈθriː wiːks ˈsælərɪ.
5 ɪmɪˈgreɪʃn ɪntə ˈbrɪtn ɪz ˈstrɪktlɪ ˈregjʊleɪtɪd.
∎

6. *It is a pity that Sheila is ill.* *
7. *Samuel Pepys was secretary of the Admiralty.* *
8. *He seized the opportunity to teach at Seattle Pacific University.* *
9. *The Harley Lyrics are a unique collection of secular and religious medieval poetry.* *
10. *Do you consider the Middle English Dictionary interesting reading?* *

■

11. *He studied medicine at Leeds, Aberdeen and Sheffield.* *
12. *His technique of saving electricity seemed extremely silly.* *
13. *Keith is reading "Wuthering Heights" by Emily Brontë.* *
14. *For reasons of hygiene, people should always keep their hands clean.* *
15. *Hey diddle diddle,*
    The cat and the fiddle,
    The cow jumped over the moon;
    The little dog laughed
    To see such sport,
    And the dish ran away with the spoon.

■

15 Front Vowel /e/

15 1 Major Allophone Drills

		Allophone	Context
15 1 1	*left, wretch, Leicester* * *thresh, jest, sweat* *	short.	/___FC
15 1 2	*web, ten, lead* * *bell, egg, tread* *	length.	/___LC

■

15 1 3 Contrast:

set : said *   *debt : dead* *   *wet : wed* *
bets : beds *   *etch : edge* *   *cess : says* *

■

6 ɪts ə ˈpɪtɪ ðət ˈʃiːləz ˈɪl.
7 ˈsæmjʊəl ˈpiːps wəz ˈsekrətrɪ əv ðɪ ˈædmɪrəltɪ.
8 hɪ ˈsiːzd ðɪ ɒpəˈtjuːnɪtɪ tə ˈtiːtʃ ət sɪˈætl pəˈsɪfɪk juːnɪˈvɜːsɪtɪ.
9 ðə ˈhɑːlɪ ˈlɪrɪks ər ə juːˈniːk kəˈlekʃn əv ˈsekjʊlər ənd rɪˈlɪdʒəs medɾiːvl ˈpəʊətrɪ.
10 dʊ jʊ kənˈsɪdə ðə ˈmɪdl ɪŋglɪʃ ˈdɪkʃənrɪ ˈɪntrəstɪŋ ˈriːdɪŋ?

■

11 hɪ ˈstʌdɪd ˈmedsɪn ət ˈliːdz, æbəˈdiːn ən ˈʃefiːld.
12 hɪz tekˈniːk əv ˈseɪvɪŋ elekˈtrɪsətɪ siːmd ɪkˈstriːmlɪ ˈsɪlɪ.
13 ˈkiːθ ɪz ˈriːdɪŋ ˈwʌðərɪŋ ˈhaɪts baɪ ˈemɪlɪ ˈbrɒntɪ.
14 fə ˈriːznz əv ˈhaɪdʒiːn, ˈpiːpl ʃʊd ˈɔːlweɪz ˈkiːp ðeə ˈhændz ˈkliːn.
15 ˈheɪ dɪdl ˈdɪdl,
ðə ˈkæt ənd ðə ˈfɪdl,
ðə ˈkaʊ dʒʌmt ˈəʊvə ðə ˈmuːn;
ðə ˈlɪtl dɒg ˈlɑːft
tə ˈsiː sʌtʃ ˈspɔːt,
ənd ðə ˈdɪʃ ræn əˈweɪ wɪð ðə ˈspuːn.

■

15

15 1

left, retʃ, ˈlestə
θreʃ, dʒest, swet
web, ten, led
bel, eg, tred

■

set : sed, det : ded, wet : wed
bets : bedz, etʃ : edʒ, ses : sez

■

15 2 Minimal Pairs
let : lit * beg : big * petty : pity * Ben : bin *
peg : pig * lessen : listen * peck : pick * well : will *
■

15 3 /e/ not /æ/!
many, any, Thames *
says, said, again *
■

15 4 For Drill Sentences see 16.

16 Front Vowel /æ/

16 1 Major Allophone Drills

	Allophone	Context
16 1 1 *latch, cat, crash ** *gap, lass, pack **	short.	/___FC
16 1 2 *jazz, ban, land ** *banged, badge, cab **	length.	/___LC

■

16 1 3 Contrast:
back : bag * slap : slab * at : add *
fat : fad * batch : badge * mat : mad *
■

16 2 Minimal Pairs
men : man * leather : lather * revel : ravel * sender : sander *
any : Annie * kettle : cattle * said : sad * wren : ran *
■

16 3 Drill Sentences
1 *What's the matter, Harold? **
2 *Anything you can do, I can do better. **
3 *Her Ascot hat was very fashionable. **
4 *Pat took her baggage to the Pan Am desk. **
5 *Sally is selling her stamp collection. **
■

15 2

let : lɪt, beg : bɪg, 'petɪ : 'pɪtɪ, ben : bɪn
peg : pɪg, 'lesn : 'lɪsn, pek : pɪk, wel : wɪl
■

15 3

'menɪ, 'enɪ, temz
sez, sed, ə'gen
■

16

16 1

lætʃ, kæt, kræʃ
gæp, læs, pæk
dʒæz, bæn, lænd
bæŋd, bædʒ, kæb
■

bæk : bæg, slæp : slæb, æt : æd
fæt : fæd, bætʃ : bædʒ, mæt : mæd
■

16 2

men : mæn, 'leðə : 'læðə, 'revl : 'rævl, 'sendə : 'sændə
'enɪ : 'ænɪ, 'ketl : 'kætl, sed : sæd, ren : ræn
■

16 3

1 'wɒts ðə 'mætə, 'hærəld?
2 'enɪθɪŋ 'juː kən 'duː, 'aɪ kən duː 'betə.
3 hər 'æskət 'hæt wəz 'verɪ 'fæʃnəbl.
4 'pæt tʊk hə 'bægɪdʒ tə ðə pæn 'æm 'desk.
5 'sælɪ ɪz 'selɪŋ hə 'stæmp kə'lekʃn.
■

6 *Geoffrey went salmon fishing, but didn't catch anything.* *

7 *Every month I get a letter from my pen pal.* *

8 *He keeps telling me about his many business contacts in Canada.*

9 *The pamphlet dealt with elementary mathematics and algebra.* *

10 *Alison got back trouble because the mattress on her bed was so bad.* *

■

11 *Sam attended a lecture on the French Revolution.* *

12 *The delegates came from Exeter, Edinburgh and Reading.* *

13 *Deborah ate bread with cherry and apple jam for breakfast.* *

14 *The American President addressed Congress in a televised speech.* *

15 *Agatha Christie's play "The Mouse Trap" has been a tremendous success.* *

■

16 *He felt that nuclear weapons should be banned.* *

17 *Let's tackle the energy problem.* *

18 *He managed to get around the rush hour traffic in Los Angeles.* *

19 *We backtracked from Land's End to Penzance.* *

20 *The Reverend Henry Ward Beecher*
   Called a hen a most elegant creature. *
   The hen, pleased with that,
   Laid an egg in his hat, −
   And thus did the hen reward Beecher. *

■

17   Central Vowel /ʌ/

17 1   Major Allophone Drills

		Allophone	Context
17 1 1	*shut, puff, chuck* * *Russ, luck, sup* *	short.	/___FC
17 1 2	*sub, bug, among* * *buzz, hugged, dull* *	length.	/___LC

■

6 ˈdʒefrɪ went ˈsæmən ˈfɪʃɪŋ, bət ˈdɪdnt ˈkætʃ enɪθɪŋ.
7 ˈevrɪ ˈmʌnθ aɪ get ə ˈletə frəm maɪ ˈpen ˈpæl.
8 hɪ ˈkiːps ˈtelɪŋ mɪ əbaʊt hɪz ˈmenɪ ˈbɪznɪs ˈkɒntækts in ˈkænədə.
9 ðə ˈpæmflət ˈdelt wɪð eləˈmentrɪ mæθəˈmætɪks ənd ˈældʒəbrə.
10 ˈælɪsn gɒt ˈbæk ˈtrʌbl bɪkɒz ðə ˈmætrəs ɒn hə ˈbed wəz ˈsəʊ ˈbæd.

■

11 ˈsæm əˈtendɪd ə ˈlektʃər ɒn ðə ˈfrenʃ revəˈluːʃn.
12 ðə ˈdeləgəts keɪm frəm ˈeksətə, ˈedɪnbərə ənd ˈredɪŋ.
13 ˈdebərə et ˈbred wɪð ˈtʃerɪ ənd ˈæpl ˈdʒæm fə ˈbrekfəst.
14 ðɪ əˈmerɪkən ˈprezədənt əˈdrest ˈkɒŋgres ɪn ə ˈteləvaɪzd ˈspiːtʃ.
15 ˈægəθə ˈkrɪstɪz ˈpleɪ ðə ˈmaʊs ˈtræp həz bɪn ə trəˈmendəs səkˈses.

■

16 hɪ ˈfelt ðət ˈnjuːklɪə ˈwepnz ʃʊd bɪ ˈbænd.
17 ˈlets ˈtækl ðɪ ˈenədʒɪ ˈprɒbləm.
18 hɪ ˈmænɪdʒd tə ˈget əraʊnd ðə ˈrʌʃ aʊə ˈtræfɪk ɪn lɒs ˈændʒəlɪs.
19 wɪ ˈbæktrækt frəm lændz ˈend tə penˈzæns.
20 ðə ˈrevərənd ˈhenrɪ wɔːd ˈbiːtʃə
kɔːld ə ˈhen ə məʊst ˈeləgənt ˈkriːtʃə.
ðə ˈhen, ˈpliːzd wɪð ˈðæt,
ˈleɪd ən ˈeg ɪn hɪz ˈhæt,
ənd ˈðʌs dɪd ðə ˈhen rɪwɔːd ˈbiːtʃə.

■

17

17 1

ʃʌt, pʌf, tʃʌk
rʌs, lʌk, sʌp
sʌb, bʌg, əˈmʌŋ
bʌz, hʌgd, dʌl

■

17 1 3 Contrast:
fuss : fuzz * cut : cud * duck : dug *
once : ones * cup : cub * luck : lug *
■

17 2 Minimal Pairs
bed : bad : bud * beck : back : buck * hell : Hal : Hull *
hem : ham : hum * pet : pat : putt * dead : Dad : dud *
■

17 3 /ʌ/ not /ɒ/!
one, once, onion, worry *
frontier, front, covet *
borough, thorough, London, oven *
■

17 4 For Drill Sentences see 20.

18 Back-Central Vowel /ɑː/

18 1 Major Allophone Drills

	Allophone	Context
18 1 1 *part, half, heart ** *bath, clerk, shark **	short.	/___FC
18 1 2 *lard, darn, cars ** *morale, balm, Mars **	length.	/___LC
18 1 3 *Shah, faux-pas, ta ** *bar, bra, hurrah ** ■	length.	/___#

18 1 4 Contrast:
staff : starve * calf : calve * mart : marred *
hart : hard * larch : large * pass : parse *
■

18 2 Minimal Pairs
stuff : staff * bun : barn * hut : heart *
hum : harm * done : darn * cull : Karl *
■

fʌs : fʌz, kʌt : kʌd, dʌk : dʌg
wʌns : wʌnz, kʌp : kʌb, lʌk : lʌg
∎

17 2

bed : bæd : bʌd, bek : bæk : bʌk, hel : hæl : hʌl
hem : hæm : hʌm, pet : pæt : pʌt, ded : dæd : dʌd
∎

17 3

wʌn, wʌns, 'ʌnjən, 'wʌrɪ
'frʌntɪə, frʌnt, 'kʌvɪt
'bʌrə, 'θʌrə, 'lʌndən, 'ʌvn
∎

18

18 1

pɑːt, hɑːf, hɑːt
bɑːθ, klɑːk, ʃɑːk
lɑːd, dɑːn, kɑːz
məˈrɑːl, bɑːm, mɑːz
ʃɑː, ˌfəʊˈpɑː, tɑː
bɑː, brɑː, hʊˈrɑː
∎

stɑːf : stɑːv, kɑːf : kɑːv, mɑːt : mɑːd
hɑːt : hɑːd, lɑːtʃ : lɑːdʒ, pɑːs : pɑːz
∎

18 2

stʌf : stɑːf, bʌn : bɑːn, hʌt : hɑːt
hʌm : hɑːm, dʌn : dɑːn, kʌl : kɑːl
∎

18 3   /ɑ:/ not /æ/!
dance, glass, pass *
can't, chance, aunt *
■

18 4   For Drill Sentences see 20.

19 Back Vowel /ɒ/

19 1   Major Allophone Drills

		Allophone	Context
19 1 1	*what, hough, loss* * *cop, yacht, off* *	short.	/___FC
19 1 2	*hog, Dodge, cod* * *job, squad, snob* * ■	length.	/___LC

19 1 3 Contrast:
pot : pod *   *lock : log* *   *boss : Boz* *
hops : Hobbes *   *knot : nod* *   *cop : cob* *
■

19 2   Minimal Pairs
cough : cuff *   *lost : lust* *   *copper : cuppa* *   *shot : shut* *
wander : wonder *   *knotty : nutty* *   *box : bucks* *
■

19 3   /ɒ/ not /ʌ/!
got, gone, cough, Coventry *
common, column, body *
■

19 4   For Drill Sentences see 20.

18 3

dɑːns, glɑːs, pɑːs
kɑːnt, tʃɑːns, ɑːnt
∎

19

19 1

wɒt, hɒk, lɒs
kɒp, jɒt, ɒf
hɒg, dɒdʒ, kɒd
dʒɒb, skwɒd, snɒb
∎

pɒt : pɒd, lɒk : lɒg, bɒs : bɒz
hɒps : hɒbz, nɒt : nɒd, kɒp : kɒb
∎

19 2

kɒf : kʌf, lɒst : lʌst, ˈkɒpə : ˈkʌpə, ʃɒt : ʃʌt
ˈwɒndə : ˈwʌndə, ˈnɒtɪ : ˈnʌtɪ, bɒks : bʌks
∎

19 3

gɒt, gɒn, kɒf, ˈkɒvəntrɪ
ˈkɒmən, ˈkɒləm, ˈbɒdɪ
∎

20 Back Vowel /ɔː/

20 1 Major Allophone Drills

	Allophone	Context
20 1 1 *court, torch, fought* * *cork, thought, walk* *	short.	/___FC
20 1 2 *stall, Ford, dawn* * *cause, board, hall* *	length.	/___LC
20 1 3 *law, core, war* * *boar, more, roar* * *Shaw, sure, shore* * ■	length.	/___#

20 1 4 Contrast:

sort : sword * *course : cores* * *bought : bored* *
wart : ward * *sauce : saws* * *horse : whores* *
■

20 2 Minimal Pairs

lord : lard * *store : star* * *port : part* *
force : farce * *taught : tart* * *author : Arthur* *
■

20 3 Drill Sentences

Listen to the following passage in its entirety.
Then drill each sentence separately.

And here's the weather forecast for tomorrow. * *Scotland will start out frosty in the morning, with a small chance of showers later on.* * *After a fairly warm start, northern England will have sunny periods with fog forming towards the middle of the afternoon.* * *Nasty fog patches are expected in much of Yorkshire and Northumberland, but apart from a little rain, it should stay mainly dry.* * *Other regions, particularly London, Dorset and Cornwall will be cloudy with occasional sunshine, and maximum temperatures will average 4 degrees centigrade.* * *Farmers in most southern parts of the country should watch out for early morning frost.* * *Strong winds will prevail along much of the coast, and gale warnings are out for small craft.* * *The outlook for Sunday and Monday:* * *A weather front will be moving up from France, causing the prospects to become hardly more encouraging.* * *And that's the lot.* * *More news at 4 o'clock.* *
■

20

20 1

kɔːt, tɔːtʃ, ˈfɔːt
kɔːk, θɔːt, wɔːk
stɔːl, fɔːd, dɔːn
kɔːz, bɔːd, hɔːl
lɔː, kɔː, wɔː
bɔː, mɔː, rɔː
ʃɔː, ʃɔː, ʃɔː

■

sɔːt : sɔːd, kɔːs : kɔːz, bɔːt : bɔːd
wɔːt : wɔːd, sɔːs : sɔːz, hɔːs : hɔːz

■

20 2

lɔːd : lɑːd, stɔː : stɑː, pɔːt : pɑːt
fɔːs : fɑːs, tɔːt : tɑːt, ˈɔːθə : ˈɑːθə

■

20 3

ænd ˈhɪəz ðə ˈweðə ˈfɔːkɑːst fə təˈmɒrəʊ. ˈskɒtlənd wɪl
ˈstɑːt aʊt ˈfrɒstɪ ɪn ðə ˈmɔːnɪŋ, wɪð ə ˈsmɔːl ˈtʃɑːns əv ˈʃaʊəz
leɪtər ˈɒn. ɑːftər ə ˈfeəlɪ ˈwɔːm ˈstɑːt, ˈnɔːðən ˈɪŋglənd wɪl hæv
ˈsʌnɪ ˈpɪərɪədz wɪð ˈfɒg ˈfɔːmɪŋ tʊwɔːdz ðə ˈmɪdl əv ðɪ ɑːftə-
ˈnuːn. ˈnɑːstɪ ˈfɒg ˈpætʃɪz ər ɪkˈspektɪd ɪn ˈmʌtʃ əv ˈjɔːkʃər
ənd nɔːˈθʌmbələnd, bət əˈpɑːt frəm ə lɪtl ˈreɪn, ɪt ʃʊd ˈsteɪ
ˈmeɪnlɪ ˈdraɪ. ˈʌðə ˈriːdʒnz, pəˈtɪkjʊləlɪ ˈlʌndən, ˈdɔːset ənd
ˈkɔːnwəl wɪl bɪ ˈklaʊdɪ wɪð əˈkeɪʒənl ˈsʌnʃaɪn, ənd ˈmæksɪməm
ˈtemprətʃəz wɪl ˈævərɪdʒ ˈfɔː dɪˈgriːz ˈsentɪgreɪd. ˈfɑːməz ɪn ˈməʊst
ˈsʌðən ˈpɑːts əv ðə ˈkʌntrɪ ʃəd ˈwɒtʃ ˈaʊt fər ˈɜːlɪ ˈmɔːnɪŋ
ˈfrɒst. ˈstrɒŋ ˈwɪndz wɪl prɪˈveɪl əlɒŋ ˈmʌtʃ əv ðə ˈkəʊst, ənd ˈgeɪl
ˈwɔːnɪŋz ər ˈaʊt fə ˈsmɔːl ˈkrɑːft. ðɪ ˈaʊtlʊk fə ˈsʌndeɪ ənd
ˈmʌndeɪ: ə ˈweðə ˈfrʌnt wɪl bɪ ˈmuːvɪŋ ˈʌp frəm ˈfrɑːns,
ˈkɔːzɪŋ ðə ˈprɒspekts tə brɪˈkʌm ˈhɑːdlɪ ˈmɔːr ɪnˈkʌrɪdʒɪŋ. ænd
ˈðæts ðə ˈlɒt. ˈmɔː ˈnjuːz ət ˈfɔːr ə ˈklɒk.

■

21   Central Vowel /ɜː/

21 1   Major Allophone Drills

		Allophone	Context
21 1 1	*curse, chirp, Burke* * *work, birth, church* *	short.	/___FC
21 1 2	*herb, third, worm* * *world, fern, sterling* *	length.	/___LC
21 1 3	*stir, fur, sir* * *prefer, blur, connoiseur* * ■	length.	/___#

21 1 4   Contrast:

Bert : bird *   *serf : serve* *   *perch : purge* *
purse : purrs *   *Curt : curd* *   *search : surge* *
■

21 2   Minimal Pairs

purred : paired *   *curr : care* *   *whirrs : wares* *
burr : bear *   *her : hair* *   *stir : stair* *
■

21 3   Drill Sentences

1 *Her purple skirt is dirty.* *
2 *Pearl is a pretty girl with curly hair.* *
3 *The birds are searching for earthworms.* *
4 *What shall I serve for dessert?* *
5 *I saw her early this year.* *
■

6 *Shirley always flirts with Bert.* *
7 *The murderer begged for mercy.* *
8 *Such impertinence is simply unheard of.* *
9 *This serves the purpose.* *
10 *The attorney was very conservative.* *
■

21

21 1

kɜ:s, tʃɜ:p, bɜ:k
wɜ:k, bɜ:θ, tʃɜ:tʃ
hɜ:b, θɜ:d, wɜ:m
wɜ:ld, fɜ:n, 'stɜ:lɪŋ
stɜ:, fɜ:, sɜ:
prə'fɜ:, blɜ:, ˌkɒnə'sɜ:
■

bɜ:t : bɜ:d, sɜ:f : sɜ:v, pɜ:tʃ : pɜ:dʒ
pɜ:s : pɜ:z, kɜ:t : kɜ:d, sɜ:tʃ : sɜ:dʒ
■

21 2

pɜ:d : peəd, kɜ: : keə, wɜ:z : weəz
bɜ: : beə, hɜ: : heə, stɜ: : steə
■

21 3

1 hə 'pɜ:pl 'skɜ:t ɪz 'dɜ:tɪ.
2 'pɜ:l ɪz ə 'prɪtɪ 'gɜ:l wɪð 'kɜ:lɪ 'heə.
3 ðə 'bɜ:dz ə 'sɜ:tʃɪŋ fər 'ɜ:θwɜ:mz.
4 'wɒt ʃəl aɪ 'sɜ:v fə dɪ'zɜ:t?
5 aɪ 'sɔ: hə 'ɜ:lɪ ðɪs 'jɪə.
■

6 'ʃɜ:lɪ 'ɔ:lweɪz 'flɜ:ts wɪð 'bɜ:t.
7 ðə 'mɜ:dərə 'begd fə 'mɜ:sɪ.
8 'sʌtʃ ɪm'pɜ:tɪnəns ɪz 'sɪmplɪ ʌn'hɜ:d 'ɒv.
9 'ðɪs 'sɜ:vz ðə 'pɜ:pəs.
10 ðɪ ə'tɜ:nɪ wəz 'verɪ kən'sɜ:vətɪv.
■

79

11 *What in the world could be worth that much work?* *
12 *Her fur coat was purchased in Heidelberg.* *
13 *The verdict was worded in no uncertain terms.* *
14 *First come, first served.* *
15 *There was a young person of Turkey,*
   Who wept when the weather was murky;
   When the day turned out fine,
   He ceased to repine,
   That capricious young person of Turkey. *
■

22 Central Vowel /ə/

22 1 Major Allophone Drills

	Allophone	Context
22 1 1 *ago, afraid, towards* * *produce, contain, forget* *	ə$_1$ ($^1/_2$ close – $^1/_2$ open)	/___C
22 1 2 *hunter, rocker, matter* * *Rhodesia, leader, Anna* *	ə$_2$ ($^1/_2$ open)	/___#

■

22 2 Some unstressed pre- and suffixes with /ə/

ad*vertisement*, be*gin*, col*lect* *
con*vert*, com*bine*, cor*rect* *
for*give*, ob*ject*, per*form* *
pro*fession*, to*gether*, pur*sue* *
re*form*, sub*tract*, pre*fer* *
■

*consider*able, *aristo*cracy, *ignor*ance *
*dist*ant, *legitim*ate, *figur*ative *
*orat*ory, *element*ary, *depend*ence *
*excell*ent, *toil*et, *relig*ious *
*aud*ible, *help*less, *chair*man *
*govern*ment, *good*ness, *theol*ogy *
*tire*some, *after*wards *
■

11 ˈwɒt ɪn ðə ˈwɜːld kʊd bɪ ˈwɜːθ ˈðæt mʌtʃ ˈwɜːk?
12 hə ˈfɜːˈkəʊt wəz ˈpɜːtʃəst ɪn ˈhaɪdlbɜːɡ.
13 ðə ˈvɜːdɪkt wəz ˈwɜːdɪd ɪn ˈnəʊ ʌnˈsɜːtn ˈtɜːmz.
14 ˈfɜːst ˈkʌm, ˈfɜːst ˈsɜːvd.
15 ðə ˈwɒz ə jʌŋ ˈpɜːsn əv ˈtɜːkɪ,
 hʊ ˈwept wen ðə ˈweðə wəz ˈmɜːkɪ;
 wen ðə ˈdeɪ tɜːnd aʊt ˈfaɪn,
 hiː ˈsiːst tə rɪˈpaɪn,
 ðæt kə prɪʃəs jʌŋ ˈpɜːsn əv ˈtɜːkɪ.

∎

22

22 1

əˈɡəʊ, əˈfreɪd, təˈwɔːdz
prəˈdjuːs, kənˈteɪn, fəˈɡet
ˈhʌntə, ˈrɒkə, ˈmætə
rəʊˈdiːʃə, ˈliːdə, ˈænə

∎

22 2

ədˈvɜːtɪsmənt, bəˈɡɪn, kəˈlekt
kənˈvɜːt, kəmˈbaɪn, kəˈrekt
fəˈɡɪv, əbˈdʒekt, pəˈfɔːm
prəˈfeʃn, təˈɡeðə, pəˈsjuː
rəˈfɔːm, səbˈtrækt, prəˈfɜː

∎

kənˈsɪdrəbl, ˌærɪˈstɒkrəsɪ, ˈɪɡnərəns
ˈdɪstənt, ləˈdʒɪtɪmət, ˈfɪɡərətɪv
ˈprətərɪ, ˌeləˈmentərɪ, dəˈpendəns
ˈeksələnt, ˈtɔɪlət, rəˈlɪdʒəs
ˈɔːdəbl, ˈhelpləs, ˈtʃeəmən
ˈɡʌvəmənt, ˈɡʊdnəs, θrˈɒlədʒɪ
ˈtaɪəsəm, ˈɑːftəwədz

∎

22 3 Some unstressed place-name elements with /ə/
*Lough*borough, *Middles*brough, *Edin*burgh *
*Lan*caster, *Ox*ford, *Birming*ham *
*Bourne*mouth, *South*wark, *Glou*cester *
■

22 4 Pronunciation of Prefixes < com-, con- >
combine, command, compose *	/ə/	/.__
conceive, conduct, concussion *		
comment, combine, comparable *	/ɒ/	/'__
concept, Concorde, conduct *		
combination, composition, commandant *	/ɒ/	/,__
condemnation, confrontation, connoisseur *		
comfort, comfy, company, compass *	/ʌ/	
conjure (to evoke a spirit), *Constable* *		

■

23 Back-Central Vowel /ʊ/

23 1 Major Allophone Drills

	Allophone	Context
23 1 1 *soot, put, puss* * *nook, bush, foot* *	short.	/__FC
23 1 2 *wool, hood, stood* * *bull, good, should* *	length.	/__LC

■

23 2 For Drill Sentences see 24.

24 Back Vowel /u:/

24 1 Major Allophone Drills

	Allophone	Context
24 1 1 *boot, juke, group* * *Zeus, truth, suit* *	short.	/__FC
24 1 2 *huge, accuse, booze* * *boob, rude, booed* *	length.	/__LC
24 1 3 *zoo, few, pooh-pooh* * *Sioux, grew, ado* *	diphth.	/__#

■

22 3

'lʌfbərə, 'mɪdlzbrə, 'ednbərə
'læŋkəstə, 'ɒksfəd, 'bɜːmɪŋəm
'bɔːnməθ, 'sʌðək, 'glɒstə
∎

22 4

kəm'baɪn, kə'mɑːnd, kəm'pəʊz
kən'siːv, kən'dʌkt, kən'kʌʃn
'kɒment, 'kɒmbaɪn, 'kɒmprəbl
'kɒnsept, 'kɒŋkɔːd, 'kɒndʌkt
ˌkɒmbɪ'neɪʃn, ˌkɒmpə'zɪʃn, ˌkɒmən'dænt
ˌkɒndem'neɪʃn, ˌkɒnfrʌn'teɪʃn, ˌkɒnə'sɜː
'kʌmfət, 'kʌmfɪ, 'kʌmpənɪ, 'kʌmpəs
'kʌndʒə, 'kʌnstəbl
∎

23

23 1

sʊt, pʊt, pʊs
nʊk, bʊʃ, fʊt
wʊl, hʊd, stʊd
bʊl, gʊd, ʃʊd
∎

24

24 1

buːt, dʒuːk, gruːp
zjuːs, truːθ, suːt
hjuːdʒ, ə'kjuːz, buːz
buːb, ruːd, buːd
zuː, ʃjuː, ˌpuː'puː
suː, gruː, ə'duː
∎

24 1 4 Contrast:
> *moot* : *mood* *   *deuce* : *dews* *   *use* (n.) : *use* (v.) *
> *cute* : *queued* *   *proof* : *prove* *   *newt* : *nude* *
>
> ∎

24 2 Minimal Pairs
> *look* : *Luke* *   *pull* : *pool* *   *full* : *fool* *
> *soot* : *suit* *   *could* : *cooed* *   *would* : *wooed* *
>
> ∎

24 3 Drill Sentences
> 1 *Sue knew how to cook the food.* *
> 2 *His beautiful new suit was all sooty.* *
> 3 *This shoe is too big for my foot.* *
> 4 *He put the poodle in the boot of his car.* *
> 5 *June went to school in Worcestershire.* *
>
> ∎
>
> 6 *A Sioux paddled his canoe down the brook.* *
> 7 *The tulips in the garden should bloom soon.* *
> 8 *The butcher was a crook.* *
> 9 *I presume that the manœuvre will prove helpful to the troops.* *
> 10 *A tutor who tooted the flute*
>   *Tried to tutor two tutors to toot.* *
>
>   *Said the two to the tutor,*
>   *"Is it harder to toot or*
>   *To tutor two tutors to toot?"* *
>
> ∎

muːt : muːd,　djuːs : djuːz,　juːs : juːz
kjuːt : kjuːd,　pruːf : pruːv,　njuːt : njuːd
∎

24 2

lʊk : luːk,　pʊl : puːl,　fʊl : fuːl
sʊt : suːt,　kʊd : kuːd,　wʊd : wuːd
∎

24 3

1　ˈsuː ˈnjuː haʊ tə ˈkʊk ðə ˈfuːd.
2　hɪz ˈbjuːtɪfʊl ˈnjuː ˈsuːt wəz ˈɔːl ˈsʊtɪ.
3　ˈðɪs ˈʃuː ɪz ˈtuː ˈbɪɡ fə maɪ ˈfʊt.
4　hɪ ˈpʊt ðə ˈpuːdl ɪn ðə ˈbuːt əv ɪz ˈkɑː.
5　ˈdʒuːn went tə ˈskuːl ɪn ˈwʊstəʃə.

∎

6　ə ˈsuː ˈpædld hɪz kəˈnuː ˈdaʊn ðə ˈbrʊk.
7　ðə ˈtjuːlɪps ɪn ðə ˈɡɑːdn ʃʊd ˈbluːm ˈsuːn.
8　ðə ˈbʊtʃə wəz ə ˈkrʊk.
9　aɪ prəˈzjuːm ðət ðə məˈnuːvə wɪl ˈpruːv ˈhelpfʊl tə ðə ˈtruːps.
10　ə ˈtjuːtə hʊ ˈtuːtɪd ðə ˈfluːt
　　traɪd tə ˈtjuːtə tuː ˈtjuːtəz tə ˈtuːt.
　　sed ðə ˈtuː tə ðə ˈtjuːtə,
　　ɪz ɪt ˈhɑːdə tə ˈtuːt ɔː
　　tə ˈtjuːtə tuː ˈtjuːtəz tə ˈtuːt.

∎

25   **Closing Diphthong /eɪ/**

25 1   Major Allophone Drills

	Allophone	Context
25 1 1 *steak, bait, eight* * *Jake, pace, ape* *	short.	/___FC
25 1 2 *afraid, feigned, gauge* * *laid, gaol, sage* *	length.	/___LC
25 1 3 *weigh, array, say* * *obey, okay, tray* * ■	length.	/___#

25 1 4   Contrast:

face : phase *   *wait : wade* *   *mace : maze* *
lace : lays *   *fate : fade* *   *pace : pays* *
■

25 2   /eɪ/ + /ə/

surveyor, greyer, player *   → /eə/
betrayal, layer, soothsayer *
■

25 3   For Drill Sentences see 27.

26   **Closing Diphthong /aɪ/**

26 1   Major Allophone Drills

	Allophone	Context
26 1 1 *fight, Paradise, rice* * *wife, pipe, Ike* *	short.	/___FC
26 1 2 *lied, arrive, eyed* * *size, abide, scribe* *	length.	/___LC
26 1 3 *fry, bye, sigh* * *wry, aye, alibi* * ■	length.	/___#

25

25 1

steɪk, beɪt, eɪt
dʒeɪk, peɪs, eɪp
əˈfreɪd, feɪnd, geɪdʒ
leɪd, dʒeɪl, seɪdʒ
weɪ, əˈreɪ, seɪ
əˈbeɪ, ˌəʊˈkeɪ, treɪ

∎

feɪs : feɪz, weɪt : weɪd, meɪs : meɪz
leɪs : leɪz, feɪt : feɪd, peɪs : peɪz

∎

25 2

səˈveɪə, ˈgreɪə, ˈpleɪə
bɪˈtreɪəl, ˈleɪə, ˈsuːθˌseɪə

∎

26

26 1

faɪt, ˈpærədaɪs, raɪs
waɪf, paɪp, aɪk
laɪd, əˈraɪv, aɪd
saɪz, əˈbaɪd, skraɪb
fraɪ, baɪ, saɪ
raɪ, aɪ, ˈælɪbaɪ

∎

26 1 4 Contrast:
> *tripe : tribe* * *bite : bide* * *wright : ride* *
> *ice : eyes* * *dice : dies* * *height : hide* *
> ■

26 2 /aɪ/+/ə/
> *choir, shire, fire* *   → /a:ə/   → /ɑ:/
> *society, dialect, quiet* *
> ■

26 3 For Drill Sentences see 27.

27 Closing Diphthong /ɔɪ/

27 1 Major Allophone Drills

		Allophone	Context
27 1 1	*oyster, coif, voice* * *Detroit, choice, joint* *	short.	/___FC
27 1 2	*poise, noise, Freud* * *foil, typhoid, Lloyd* *	length.	/___LC
27 1 3	*annoy, Troy, enjoy* * *Savoy, buoy, Illinois* *	length.	/___#

■

27 1 4 Contrast:
> *Joyce : joys** *quoit : coy* * *Boyce : boys* *
> ■

27 2 /ɔɪ/+/ə/
> *employer, enjoyable, destroyer* * → /ɔ:ə/
> *joyous, annoyance, royal* *
> ■

27 3 Drill Sentences
1. *Try it, you'll like it.* *
2. *He coined a new phrase.* *
3. *My wife's diary is strictly private.* *
4. *The rain in Spain stays mainly in the plain.* *
5. *Mind your own business, Iris.* *

■

traɪp : traɪb, baɪt : baɪd, raɪt : raɪd
aɪs : aɪz, daɪs : daɪz, haɪt : haɪd
∎

26 2

ˈkwaɪə, ˈʃaɪə, ˈfaɪə
səˈsaɪətɪ, ˈdaɪəlekt, ˈkwaɪət
∎

27

27 1

ˈɔɪstə, kɔɪf, vɔɪs
dɪˈtrɔɪt, tʃɔɪs, dʒɔɪnt
pɔɪz, nɔɪz, frɔɪd
fɔɪl, ˈtaɪfɔɪd, lɔɪd
əˈnɔɪ, trɔɪ, enˈdʒɔɪ
səˈvɔɪ, bɔɪ, ˌɪlɪˈnɔɪ
∎

dʒɔɪs : dʒɔɪz, kɔɪt : kɔɪ, bɔɪs : bɔɪz
∎

27 2

ɪmˈplɔɪə, ɪnˈdʒɔɪəbl, dɪˈstrɔɪə
ˈdʒɔɪəs, əˈnɔɪəns, ˈrɔɪəl
∎

27 3

1 ˈtraɪ ɪt, juːl ˈlaɪk ɪt.
2 hɪ ˈkɔɪnd ə njuː ˈfreɪz.
3 maɪ ˈwaɪfs ˈdaɪərɪ ɪz ˈstrɪktlɪ ˈpraɪvət.
4 ðə ˈreɪn ɪn ˈspeɪn steɪz ˈmeɪnlɪ ɪn ðə ˈpleɪn.
5 ˈmaɪnd jɔːr ˈəʊn ˈbɪznɪs, ˈaɪərɪs.
∎

6 *The boys liked the oysters.* *

7 *Why do you always fight?* *

8 *What's your name?* *

9 *Shame on you.* *

10 *There was a young lady of Niger
Who smiled as she rode on a tiger;* *
  *They returned from the ride
  With the lady inside,
  And the smile on the face of the tiger.* *

■

11 *He joined the Boy Scouts.* *

12 *It's time you made up your mind.* *

13 *What a strange relationship.* *

14 *You scream, I scream, we all scream for ice-cream.* *

15 *"Love's Labour's Lost" is the name of one of
Shakespeare's plays.* *

■

16 *See you later, alligator – in a while, crocodile.* *

17 *We'll wait till doomsday.* *

18 *There was a young fellow named Tate
Who dined with his girl at 8.08;* *
  *But I'd hate to relate
  What that fellow named Tate
  And his tête-à-tête ate at 8.08.* *

19 *These pronunciation exercises are a pain in the neck.* *

■

20 Listen to the following dialogue in its entirety.
Then drill each sentence separately.

  A: (Dialling) *Eight – five – nine – five – eight.* *

  B: *Eight-five-nine-five-eight.* * *Bailey speaking.* *

  A: *This is Mrs. Clayton from Tyler's Lane.* * *I'd like to complain to Mr. Foyles.* *

  B: *I'm afraid there is no Mr. Foyles in this place.* *

  A: *No Mr. Foyles?* * *Who else made me buy that stupid radio last Friday?* * *I can't make it play.* *

6 ðə 'bɔɪz 'laɪkt ðɪ 'ɔɪstəz.
7 'waɪ də ju 'ɔːlweɪz 'faɪt?
8 'wɒts jɔː 'neɪm?
9 'ʃeɪm ɒn juː.
10 ðə 'wɒz ə jʌŋ 'leɪdi əv 'naɪgə
    hu 'smaɪld əz ʃɪ 'rəʊd ɒn ə 'taɪgə.
    ðeɪ rɪ'tɜːnd frəm ðə 'raɪd
    wɪð ðə 'leɪdɪ ɪn'saɪd,
    ənd ðə 'smaɪl ɒn ðə 'feɪs əv ðə 'taɪgə.

■

11 hi 'dʒɔɪnd ðə bɔɪ 'skaʊts.
12 ɪts 'taɪm ju 'meɪd 'ʌp jɔː 'maɪnd.
13 'wɒt ə 'streɪndʒ rɪ'leɪʃnʃɪp.
14 'juː 'skriːm, 'aɪ 'skriːm, wɪ 'ɔːl 'skriːm fə 'aɪskriːm.
15 'lʌvz 'leɪbəz 'lɒst ɪz ðə 'neɪm əv 'wʌn əv
    'ʃeɪkspɪəz 'pleɪz.

■

16 'siː ju 'leɪtər, 'æləgeɪtə – ɪn ə 'waɪl, 'krɒkədaɪl.
17 wiːl 'weɪt tɪl 'duːzdeɪ.
18 ðə 'wɒz ə jʌŋ 'feləʊ neɪmd 'teɪt
    hu 'daɪnd wɪð ɪz 'gɜːl ət eɪt 'eɪt;
    bət aɪd 'heɪt tə rɪ'leɪt
    wɒt ðæt 'feləʊ neɪmd 'teɪt
    ənd hɪz 'teɪt ə teɪt 'eɪt ət eɪt 'eɪt.
19 'ðiːz prənʌnsɪ'eɪʃn 'eksəsaɪzɪz ər ə 'peɪn ɪn ðə 'nek.

■

20

    eɪ : (daɪəlɪŋ) 'eɪt faɪv 'naɪn 'faɪv 'eɪt.
    biː : 'eɪt faɪv 'naɪn faɪv 'eɪt. 'beɪlɪ 'spiːkɪŋ.
    eɪ : 'ðɪs ɪz 'mɪsɪz 'kleɪtn frəm 'taɪləz 'leɪn. aɪd 'laɪk tə
        kəm'pleɪn tə mɪstə 'fɔɪlz.
    biː : aɪm ə'freɪd ðəz nəʊ mɪstə 'fɔɪlz ɪn ðɪs 'pleɪs.
    eɪ : 'nəʊ mɪstə 'fɔɪlz? 'huː 'els meɪd mɪ 'baɪ 'ðæt 'stjuːpɪd
        'reɪdɪəʊ 'lɑːst 'fraɪdeɪ? aɪ 'kɑːnt meɪk ɪt 'pleɪ.

91

B: *I have no idea. * Are you sure you dialled the right number? **

A: *Of course I am. * Five-eight-nine-five-eight. * This is most annoying. * Why are you trying to confuse me? **

B: *Patience, Madame. * I'm sure we can clear up this mistake. * You say you dialled five-eight-nine-five-eight? **

A: *Quite right. * And for the last time, where is Mr. Foyles? **

B: *Now listen, Mrs. Clayton. * My number is eight-five-nine-five-eight, not five-eight-nine-five-eight. * My name is Roy Bailey, and I have no radios for sale. * By the way, have you tried plugging it in? * Good day. **

■

28   Closing Diphthong /aʊ/

28 1   Major Allophone Drills

	Allophone	Context
28 1 1 *pout, house, couch ** *out, mouth, Faust **	short.	/___FC
28 1 2 *arouse, spouse, ground ** *scrounge, town, fowl **	length.	/___LC
28 1 3 *cow, mow, Slough ** *thou, wow, plough ** ■	length.	/___#

28 1 4 Contrast:

lout : loud * bout : bowed * kraut : crowd * house (n.) *: house* (v.) ***

■

28 2   /aʊ/ + /ə/

coward, tower, sour * *our, power, nowadays **	→ /a:ə/ → /ɑ:/	/ ~
vowel, towel, bowel *	/aʊ(ə)/	/___l

■

28 3   For Drill Sentences see 29.

bi: : aɪ hæv ˈnəʊ aɪˈdɪə. ˈɑ: jʊ ˈʃɔ: jʊ ˈdaɪəld ðə ˈraɪt ˈnʌmbə?

eɪ : ɔf ˈkɔːs aɪ ˈæm. ˈfaɪv eɪt ˈnaɪn faɪv ˈeɪt. ðɪs ɪz ˈməʊst əˈnɔɪɪŋ. ˈwaɪ ə jʊ ˈtraɪɪŋ tə kənˈfjuːz mɪ?

bi: : ˈpeɪʃns ˈmædəm. aɪm ˈʃɔ: wɪ kən ˈklɪər ˈʌp ðɪs mɪˈsteɪk. jʊ ˈseɪ jʊ ˈdaɪəld ˈfaɪv eɪt ˈnaɪn faɪv ˈeɪt?

eɪ : ˈkwaɪt ˈraɪt. ənd fə ðə ˈlɑːst ˈtaɪm, ˈweər ɪz mɪstə ˈfɔɪlz.

bi: : naʊ ˈlɪsn, mɪsɪz ˈkleɪtn. maɪ ˈnʌmbər ɪz eɪt ˈfaɪv ˈnaɪn faɪv ˈeɪt, ˈnɒt faɪv ˈeɪt ˈnaɪn faɪv ˈeɪt. maɪ ˈneɪm ɪz ˈrɔɪ ˈbeɪlɪ, ənd aɪ ˈhæv nəʊ ˈreɪdɪəʊz fə ˈseɪl. ˈbaɪ ðə ˈweɪ, ˈhæv jʊ ˈtraɪd ˈplʌgɪŋ ɪt ˈɪn? gʊd ˈdeɪ.

■

28

28 1

paʊt, haʊs, kaʊtʃ
aʊt, maʊθ, faʊst
əˈraʊz, spaʊz, graʊnd
skraʊndʒ, taʊn, faʊl
kaʊ, maʊ, slaʊ
ðaʊ, waʊ, plaʊ
■

laʊt : laʊd, baʊt : baʊd, kraʊt : kraʊd
haʊs : haʊz
■

28 2

ˈkaʊəd, ˈtaʊə, ˈsaʊə
ˈaʊə, ˈpaʊə, ˈnaʊədeɪz
ˈvaʊəl, ˈtaʊəl, ˈbaʊəl
■

29 Closing Diphthong /əʊ/

29 1 Major Allophone Drills

	Allophone	Context
29 1 1 *goat, hoax, yolk* * *brooch, betroth, gauche* *	short.	/___FC
29 1 2 *nose, rose, load* * *Job, mauve, gold* *	length.	/___LC
29 1 3 *sew, apropos, foe* * *although, toe, Joe* *	length.	/___#

∎

29 1 4 Contrast:

dose : doze * *close* (n.) : *close* (v.) * *boat : bode* *
rote : rode * *broke : brogue* * *gross : grows* *
∎

29 2 /əʊ/ + /ə/

slower, mower, lower *   → /ɜː/
grower, sewer, blower *
∎

29 3 Drill Sentences

1 *Slow down, I can't follow.* *
2 *Her account showed two thousand pounds.* *
3 *I don't know anything about it.* *
4 *The Tower of London is very renowned.* *
5 *This is a poem by Alexander Pope.* *
∎

6 *We proudly announce our success.* *
7 *This is no joke.* *
8 *I can't pronounce this vowel.* *
9 *Is Joseph going to Poland?* *
10 *Working more than ten hours a day is not allowed.* *
∎

29

29 1

gəʊt, həʊks, jəʊk
brəʊtʃ, bɪˈtrəʊθ, gəʊʃ
nəʊz, rəʊz, ləʊd
dʒəʊb, məʊv, gəʊld
səʊ, ˌæprəˈpəʊ, fəʊ
ɔːlˈðəʊ, təʊ, dʒəʊ
■

dəʊs : dəʊz,   kləʊs : kləʊz,   bəʊt : bəʊd
rəʊt : rəʊd,   brəʊk : brəʊg,   grəʊs : grəʊz
■

29 2

ˈsləʊə, ˈməʊə, ˈləʊə
ˈgrəʊə, ˈsəʊə, ˈbləʊə
■

29 3

1 ˈsləʊ ˈdaʊn, aɪ ˈkɑːnt ˈfɒləʊ.
2 hər əˈkaʊnt ʃəʊd ˈtuː ˈθaʊznd ˈpaʊndz.
3 aɪ ˈdəʊnt nəʊ ˈenɪθɪŋ əˈbaʊt ɪt.
4 ðə ˈtaʊər əv ˈlʌndən ɪz ˈverɪ rɪˈnaʊnd.
5 ˈðɪs ɪz ə ˈpəʊəm baɪ æleɡˈzɑːndə ˈpəʊp.
■

6 wɪ ˈpraʊdlɪ əˈnaʊns ɑː səkˈses.
7 ˈðɪs ɪz ˈnəʊ ˈdʒəʊk.
8 aɪ ˈkɑːnt prəˈnaʊns ðɪs ˈvaʊəl.
9 ɪz ˈdʒəʊzɪf ˈɡəʊɪŋ tə ˈpəʊlənd?
10 ˈwɜːkɪŋ ˈmɔː ðən ˈten aʊəz ə ˈdeɪ ɪz ˈnɒt əˈlaʊd.
■

11 *Petroleum is also known as Black Gold.* *
12 *The county suffered from a severe drought.* *
13 *They were hoping for a Socialist coalition.* *
14 *I'm being swallowed by a boa constrictor.* *
15 *On her birthday, flowers were literally showered upon her.* *
∎

16 *Joan almost failed her O-levels.* *
17 *Water power is essential for our town.* *
18 *The show is over.* *
19 *There is no doubt about his whereabouts.* *
20 *Moses supposes his toeses are roses,*
    But Moses supposes erroneously; *
    For nobody's toeses are posies of roses,
    As Moses supposes his toeses to be. *
∎

30   Centring Diphthong /ɪə/

30 1   Major Allophone Drills

		Allophone	Context
30 1 1	*pierce, fierce* *	short.	/___FC
30 1 2	*beard, real, weird* *	length.	/___LC
30 1 3	*sheer, near, queer* *	length.	/___#
	grenadier, beer, rear *		

∎

30 1 4 *funniest, Indian, Namibia* *   /.___
        bastion, Zambia, venereal *
∎

30 1 5 Contrast:
        pierce : peers *   *Peart : Peard* *   *tierce : tears* *   *fierce : fears* *
∎

30 2   For Drill Sentences see 32.

11 pəˈtrəʊljəm ɪz ˈɔːlsəʊ ˈnəʊn əz ˈblæk ˈɡəʊld.
12 ðə ˈkaʊntɪ ˈsʌfəd frəm ə səˈvɪə ˈdraʊt.
13 ðeɪ wə ˈhəʊpɪŋ fər ə ˈsəʊʃəlɪst kəʊəˈlɪʃn.
14 ˈaɪm biːɪŋ ˈswɒləʊd baɪ ə ˈbəʊə kənˈstrɪktə.
15 ɒn hə ˈbɜːθdeɪ ˈflaʊəz wə ˈlɪtrəlɪ ʃaʊəd əpɒn hə.
∎

16 dʒəʊn ˈɔːlməʊst ˈfeɪld hər ˈəʊlevlz.
17 ˈwɔːtə paʊər ɪz ɪˈsenʃl fər aʊə ˈtaʊn.
18 ðə ˈʃəʊ ɪz ˈəʊvə.
19 ðəz ˈnəʊ ˈdaʊt əbaʊt hɪz ˈweərəbaʊts.
20 ˈməʊzɪz səˈpəʊzɪz hɪz ˈtəʊzɪz ə ˈrəʊzɪz,
   bət ˈməʊzɪz səˈpəʊzɪz ɪˈrəʊnjəslɪ;
   fə ˈnəʊbədɪz ˈtəʊzɪz ə ˈpəʊzɪz əv ˈrəʊzɪz,
   əz ˈməʊzɪz səˈpəʊzɪz hɪz ˈtəʊzɪz tə ˈbiː.
∎

30

30 1

pɪəs, fɪəs
bɪəd, rɪəl, wɪəd
ʃɪə, nɪə, kwɪə
ˌɡrenəˈdɪə, bɪə, rɪə
∎

ˈfʌnɪəst, ˈɪndɪən, nəˈmɪbɪə
ˈbæstɪən, ˈzæmbɪə, vəˈnɪərɪəl
∎

pɪəs : pɪəz, pɪət : pɪəd, tɪəs : tɪəz, fɪəs : fɪəz
∎

31   Centring Diphthong /eə/

31 1   Major Allophone Drills

		Allophone	Context
31 1 1	*scarce* *	short.	/__FC
31 1 2	*fares, aired, shares* *	length.	/__LC
31 1 3	*mayor, ware, pear* * *prayer, lair, beware* * ∎	length.	/__#

31 2   Minimal Pairs

fear : fair *   *Lear : lair* *   *here : hare* *
tier : tear *   *sheer : share* *   *peering : paring* *
merry : Mary *   *very : vary* *   *ferry : fairy* *
marry : Mary *   *carry : Carey* *
∎

31 3   For Drill Sentences see 32.

32   Centring Diphthong /ʊə/

32 1   Major Allophone Drills

Allophone   Context

32 1 1   *truant, jewel, fluent* *
         bluer, fewer, cruel *

32 1 2   *virtuous, influence, continuous* *   /.__
         manual, valuable, vacuum *
         ∎

32 1 3   *your, sure, pure* *   → /ɔː/   / < our, ur(e),
         during, Europe, poor *   eur, oor >
         ∎

31

31 1

skeəs
feəz, eəd, ʃeəz
meə, weə, peə
preə, leə, bə'weə
■

31 2

fıə : feə, lıə : leə, hıə : heə
tıə : teə, ʃıə : ʃeə, 'pıərıŋ : 'peərıŋ
'merı : 'meərı, 'verı : 'veərı, 'ferı : 'feərı
'mærı : 'meərı, 'kærı : 'keərı
■

32

32 1

truənt, dʒuəl, fluənt
bluə, fjuə, kruəl
'vɜːtʃuəs, 'ınfluəns, kən'tınjuəs
'mænjuəl, 'væljuəbl, 'vækjuəm
■

juə, ʃuə, pjuə
'djuərıŋ, 'juərəp, puə
■

2 Drill Sentences

1. *I don't care too much for air-conditioning.* *
2. *He nearly forgot to buy some beer.* *
3. *Muriel was furious.* *
4. *Beware of the dog.* *
5. *The atmosphere was really eerie.* *

■

6. *Curiosity killed the cat.* *
7. *The stairs were very narrow.* *
8. *We're clearly in arrears.* *
9. *Don't be so immature.* *
10. *This is terribly unfair.* *

■

11. *Here you are.* *
12. *Surely, you're not afraid of tourists.* *
13. *You can play solitaire anywhere.* *
14. *Are Nigeria and Liberia in the southern hemisphere?* *
15. *The European community is supposed to ensure greater economic security.* *

■

16. *They repaired their aquarium.* *
17. *Stop interfering!* *
18. *Cruelty to animals is detestable behaviour.* *
19. *We're merely pretending.* *
20. *The curate was as poor as a church mouse.* *

■

21. *There were quite a few bears in the area.* *
22. *His tears were sincere.* *
23. *This paper has fewer caricatures than I thought.* *
24. *He was chairman for a year.* *
25. *I fear his ideas are not very convincing.* *

■

32 2

1 aɪ dəʊnt ˈkeə tuː ˈmʌtʃ fər ˈeəkəndɪʃnɪŋ.
2 hɪ ˈnɪəlɪ fəˈɡɒt tə ˈbaɪ səm ˈbɪə.
3 ˈmjʊərɪəl wəz ˈfjʊərɪəs.
4 bɪˈweər əv ðə ˈdɒɡ.
5 ðɪ ˈætməsfɪə wəz ˈrɪəlɪ ˈɪərɪ.

■

6 kjʊərɪˈɒsətɪ ˈkɪld ðə ˈkæt.
7 ðə ˈsteəz wə ˈverɪ ˈnærəʊ.
8 wɪə ˈklɪəlɪ ɪn əˈrɪəz.
9 ˈdəʊnt bɪ səʊ ɪməˈtjʊə.
10 ˈðɪs ɪz ˈterɪblɪ ʌnˈfeə.

■

11 ˈhɪə jʊ ˈɑː.
12 ˈʃɔːlɪ, jʊə nɒt əˈfreɪd əv ˈtʊərɪsts.
13 jʊ kən ˈpleɪ ˈsɒlɪteər ˈenɪweə.
14 ɑː naɪˈdʒɪərɪə ənd laɪˈbɪərɪə ɪn ðə ˈsʌðən ˈhemɪsfɪə?
15 ðə jʊərəˈpɪən kəmˈjuːnətɪ ɪz səˈpəʊzd tʊ ɪnˈʃɔː ˈɡreɪtər ekəˈnɒmɪk səˈkjʊərətɪ.

■

16 ðeɪ rɪˈpeəd ðeər əˈkweərɪəm.
17 ˈstɒp ɪntəˈfɪərɪŋ.
18 ˈkrʊəltɪ tʊ ˈænɪmlz ɪz dɪˈtestəbl bɪˈheɪvjə.
19 wɪə ˈmɪəlɪ prɪˈtendɪŋ.
20 ðə ˈkjʊərət wəz əz ˈpʊər əz ə ˈtʃɜːtʃ ˈmaʊs.

■

21 ðə wə ˈkwaɪt ə ˈfjuː ˈbeəz ɪn ðɪ ˈeərɪə.
22 hɪz ˈtɪəz wə sɪnˈsɪə.
23 ˈðɪs ˈpeɪpə hæz ˈfjuə ˈkærɪkətjʊəz ðən aɪ ˈθɔːt.
24 hɪ wəz ˈtʃeəmən fər ə ˈjɪə.
25 aɪ ˈfɪə hɪz aɪˈdɪəz ə ˈnɒt ˈverɪ kənˈvɪnsɪŋ.

■

26 *Her jewelry box was newer than mine.* *
27 *The librarian ordered various books for the library.* *
28 *These criteria were nearly overlooked.* *
29 *Who would volunteer to go to Siberia?* *
∎

30 Listen to the following passage in its entirety. Then drill each sentence separately.
   A: *Could you lend Sarah a pair of boots, by any chance?* * *She's preparing a walking tour in the Lake District, and she says she can't wear hers any more.* *
   B: *A walking tour!* * *Can she be serious?* * *Not in this weather, surely!* * *But if she really wants to, I do have a spare pair she could borrow.* *
   A: *Well, when I first heard about this latest idea of hers my hair stood on end, too.* * *Sheer madness, I think.* * *And my poor parents, of course, nearly fainted.* * *But she doesn't care.* *
   B: *Anything particular that makes her go up there?* *
   A: *I'm not sure.* * *She told my parents she wanted to follow in Wordsworth's footsteps: Grasmere, Windermere and so on, you know.* * *But to me her newly discovered love of the Romantics is somewhat suspect.* * *Who knows what she's up to.* *

∎

26 ˈhɜː ˈdʒuəlrɪ ˈbɒks wəz ˈnjuə ðən ˈmaɪn.
27 ðə laɪˈbreərɪən ɔːdəd ˈveərɪəs ˈbʊks fə ðə ˈlaɪbrərɪ.
28 ˈðiːz kraɪˈtɪərɪə wə ˈnɪəlɪ əʊvəˈlʊkt.
29 ˈhuː wʊd vɒlənˈtɪə tə ˈgəʊ tə saɪˈbɪərɪə?

∎

30

eɪ: kʊd ju ˈlend ˈseərə ə peər əv ˈbuːts, baɪ ˈenɪ ˈtʃɑːns?
ʃiːz prɪˈpeərɪŋ ə ˈwɔːkɪŋ tʊər ɪn ðə ˈleɪk ˈdɪstrɪkt, ənd
ʃɪ ˈsez ʃɪ kɑːnt ˈweə ˈhɜːz enɪ mɔː.

biː: ə ˈwɔːkɪŋ ˈtʊə! ˈkæn ʃɪ bɪ ˈsɪərɪəs? ˈnɒt ɪn ˈðɪs
ˈweðə, ˈʃɔːlɪ! bət ɪf ʃɪ ˈrɪəlɪ ˈwɒnts ˈtʊ, aɪ ˈduː
ˈhæv ə ˈspeə ˈpeə ʃɪ kəd ˈbɒrəʊ.

eɪ: wel, wen ˈaɪ fɜːst ˈhɜːd əbaʊt ðɪs ˈleɪtɪst aɪˈdɪər əv ˈhɜːz
maɪ ˈheə stʊd ɒn ˈend, ˈtuː. ˈʃɪə ˈmædnəs, aɪ ˈθɪŋk.
ənd maɪ ˈpɔː ˈpeərənts əf kɔːs, ˈnɪəlɪ ˈfeɪntɪd. bət ˈʃiː
dʌznt ˈkeə.

biː: ˈenɪθɪŋ pəˈtɪkjʊlə ðət ˈmeɪks hə gəʊ ˈʌp ˈðeə?

eɪ: aɪm ˈnɒt ˈʃɔː. ʃɪ ˈtəʊld maɪ ˈpeərənts ʃɪ ˈwɒntɪd tə ˈfɒləʊ
ɪn ˈwɜːdzwəθs ˈfʊtsteps, ˈgrɑːsmɪə, ˈwɪndəmɪər ənd ˈsəʊ
ɒn, jʊ ˈnəʊ. bət tə ˈmiː hə ˈnjuːlɪ dɪˈskʌvəd ˈlʌv əv
ðə rəʊˈmæntɪks ɪz ˈsʌmwɒt ˈsʌspekt. ˈhuː nəʊz ˈwɒt
ʃiːz ˈʌp ˈtʊ.

∎

33 Word Stress

33 1 Major Stress Patterns

	pattern
Monday, ballet, famous *	'1 - 2
cigar, hotel, prefer *	1 - '2
violin, Chinese, canteen *	,1 - '2
energy, communist, Arabic *	'1 - 2 - 3
suspicious, strategic, Arabian *	1 - '2 - 3
cigarette, engineer, refugee *	,1 - 2 - '3
admirable, comfortably, personally *	'1 - 2 - 3 - 4
philosophy, ridiculous, catastrophe *	1 - '2 - 3 - 4
scientific, disproportion, politician *	,1 - 2 - '3 - 4
Protestantism, criticizable *	'1 - 2 - 3 - 4 - 5
Catholicism, considerable, particularly *	1 - '2 - 3 - 4 - 5
aristocracy, mathematical, possibility *	,1 - 2 - '3 - 4 - 5
pasteurization, characteristic *	,1 - 2 - 3 - '4 - 5
pronunciation, consideration *	1 - ,2 - 3 - '4 - 5
transformationally, photographically *	,1 - 2 - '3 - 4 - 6 - 6
nationalization, characterization *	,1 - 2 - 3 - 4 - '5 - 6
inferiority, bacteriologist *	1 - ,2 - 3 - '4 - 5 - 6

■

33 2 Contrast:

reform : *reformation,*   *suppose* : *supposition* *
admire : *admiration,*   *prepare* : *preparation* *
political : *politician,*   *photography* : *photographic* *

■

33 3 Double Stress

archbishop, shop-window, good-looking *
week-end, outside, double-cross *
home-rule, College House, Town Hall *
Victoria Station, Chesterton Road *

■

33

33 1

ˈmʌndeɪ, ˈbæleɪ, ˈfeɪməs
sɪˈgɑː, həʊˈtel, prəˈfɜː
ˌvaɪəˈlɪn, ˌtʃaɪˈniːz, ˌkænˈtiːn
ˈenədʒɪ, ˈkɒmjʊnɪst, ˈærəbɪk
səˈspɪʃəs, strəˈtiːdʒɪk, əˈreɪbjən
ˌsɪgəˈret, ˌendʒɪˈnɪə, ˌrefjʊˈdʒiː
ˈædmərəbl, ˈkʌmfətəbli, ˈpɜːsənəlɪ
fɪˈlɒsəfɪ, rɪˈdɪkjʊləs, kəˈtæstrəfɪ
ˌsaɪənˈtɪfɪk, ˌdɪsprəˈpɔːʃn, ˌpɒlɪˈtɪʃn
ˈprɒtəstəntɪzm, ˈkrɪtɪsaɪzəbl
kəˈθɒlɪsɪzm, kənˈsɪdərəbl, pəˈtɪkjʊləlɪ
ˌærɪˈstɒkrəsɪ, ˌmæθəˈmætɪkl, ˌpɒsəˈbɪlətɪ
ˌpɑːstəraɪˈzeɪʃn, ˌkærəktəˈrɪstɪk
prəˌnʌnsɪˈeɪʃn, kənˌsɪdəˈreɪʃn
ˌtrænsfəˈmeɪʃənəlɪ, ˌfəʊtəˈgræfɪkəlɪ
ˌnæʃənəlaɪˈzeɪʃn, ˌkærəktəraɪˈzeɪʃn
ɪnˌfɪərɪˈɒrətɪ, bækˌtɪərɪˈɒlədʒɪst

∎

33 2

rəˈfɔːm : ˌrefəˈmeɪʃn, səˈpəʊz : ˌsʌpəˈzɪʃn
ədˈmaɪə : ˌædməˈreɪʃn, prəˈpeə : ˌprepəˈreɪʃn
pəˈlɪtɪkl : ˌpɒlɪˈtɪʃn, fəˈtɒgrəfɪ : ˌfəʊtəˈgræfɪk

∎

33 3

ˌɑːtʃˈbɪʃəp, ʃɒp ˈwɪndəʊ, ˌgʊd ˈlʊkɪŋ
ˌwiːk ˈend, ˌaʊtˈsaɪd, ˌdʌbl ˈkrɒs
ˌhəʊm ˈruːl, ˌkɒlɪdʒ ˈhaʊs, ˌtaʊn ˈhɔːl
vɪkˌtɔːrɪə ˈsteɪʃn, ˌtʃestətən ˈrəʊd

∎

33 4 Contrast:
Hyde Park : Hyde Park Corner *
Guild Hall : near Guild Hall *
sixteen : sweet sixteen *
plum-pudding : good plum-pudding *
second-hand : second-hand furniture *
■

33 5 Contrast:
an overlap : to overlap *   *an insult : to insult* *
a protest : to protest *   *an insight : to incite* *
a combine : to combine *   *a conduct : to conduct* *
a convert : to convert *   *an increase : to increase* *
a suspect : to suspect *   *a rebel : to rebel* *
■

33 6 Drill Sentences
1 *I'd like to become an English teacher.* *
2 *The headmaster objected to an English teacher of Russian.* *
3 *The books he returned had too many dog's-ears.* *
4 *My dog's ears had to be clipped.* *
5 *If you turn on the light in the dark room it isn't a dark room any longer.* *
■

6 *She served the meal on a hot plate.* *
7 *My hot plate blew a fuse.* *
8 *Our next door neighbour died last month.* *
9 *He lived next door.* *
10 *They received their just deserts.* *
■

11 *The plane crashed on a desert island.* *
12 *What's for dessert today?* *
13 *Her set smile did not once desert her.* *
14 *She contracted German measles.* *
15 *The film-star was offered a three year contract.* *
■

33 4

ˌhaɪd ˈpɑːk : ˈhaɪd pɑːk ˈkɔːnə
ˌɡɪld ˈhɔːl : ˈnɪə ɡɪld ˈhɔːl
ˌsɪksˈtiːn : ˈswiːt sɪksˈtiːn
ˌplʌm ˈpʊdɪŋ : ˈɡʊd plʌm ˈpʊdɪŋ
ˌseknd ˈhænd : ˈseknd hænd ˈfɜːnɪtʃə
■

33 5

ən ˈəʊvəlæp : tʊ ˌəʊvəˈlæp, ən ˈɪnsʌlt : tʊ ɪnˈsʌlt
ə ˈprəʊtest : tə prəʊˈtest, ən ˈɪnsaɪt : tʊ ɪnˈsaɪt
ə ˈkɒmbaɪn : tə kəmˈbaɪn, ə ˈkɒndʌkt : tə kənˈdʌkt
ə ˈkɒnvɜːt : tə kənˈvɜːt, ən ˈɪnkriːs : tʊ ɪnˈkriːs
ə ˈsʌspekt : tə səsˈpekt, ə ˈrebl : tə rɪˈbel
■

33 6

1 aɪd ˈlaɪk tə bɪˈkʌm ən ˈɪŋglɪʃ tiːtʃə.
2 ðə hedˈmɑːstər əbˈdʒektɪd tʊ ən ˈɪŋglɪʃ ˈtiːtʃər əv ˈrʌʃn.
3 ðə ˈbʊks hɪ rɪˈtɜːnd hæd ˈtuː menɪ ˈdɒɡz ɪəz.
4 maɪ ˈdɒɡz ˈɪəz hæd tə bɪ ˈklɪpt.
5 ɪf jʊ ˈtɜːn ˈɒn ðə ˈlaɪt ɪn ðə ˈdɑːk ruːm ɪt ɪznt ə ˈdɑːk ˈruːm enɪ ˈlɒŋɡə.

■

6 ʃɪ ˈsɜːvd ðə ˈmiːl ɒn ə ˈhɒt ˈpleɪt.
7 maɪ ˈhɒt pleɪt ˈbluː ə ˈfjuːz.
8 ɑː ˈneks dɔː ˈneɪbə ˈdaɪd lɑːst ˈmʌnθ.
9 hɪ ˈlɪvd neks ˈdɔː.
10 ðeɪ rəˈsiːvd ðeə ˈdʒʌst dɪˈzɜːts.

■

11 ðə ˈpleɪn ˈkræʃt ɒn ə ˈdezət ˈaɪlənd.
12 ˈwɒts fə dɪˈzɜːt təˈdeɪ?
13 hə ˈset ˈsmaɪl dɪd nɒt ˈwʌns dɪˈzɜːt hə.
14 ʃɪ kənˈtræktɪd ˈdʒɜːmən ˈmiːzlz.
15 ðə ˈfɪlm stɑː wəz ˈɒfəd ə ˈθriː jɜː ˈkɒntrækt.

■

16 *They refused to concrete the pavement.* *
17 *The refuse wasn't collected for weeks.* *
18 *These are nice prospects.* *
19 *The prospectors prospected for gold.* *
20 *He frequently consulted the doctor.* *

■

21 *This beach isn't much frequented.* *
22 *Our thermometer records the temperature in centigrade.* *
23 *The conductor's conduct was quite improper.* *
24 *The magazine conducted a survey.* *
25 *Several new converts joined the church.* *

■

26 *How do you convert meters into inches?* *
27 *He was doing research in rhetoric.* *
28 *Arithmetic and trigonometry were his favourite academic subjects.* *
29 *On the contrary, I find her quite admirable.* *
30 *Mary, Mary, quite contrary,*
   How does your garden grow?
   With silver bells and cockle shells,
   And pretty maids all in a row. *

■

16 ðeɪ rɪˈfjuːzd tə ˈkɒnkriːt ðə ˈpeɪvmənt.
17 ðə ˈrefjuːs wɒznt kəˈlektɪd fə ˈwiːks.
18 ˈðiːz ə ˈnaɪs ˈprɒspekts.
19 ðə prəˈspektəz prəˈspektɪd fə ˈɡəʊld.
20 hɪ ˈfriːkwəntlɪ kənˈsʌltɪd ðə ˈdɒktə.

∎

21 ˈðɪs ˈbiːtʃ ɪznt ˈmʌtʃ frɪˈkwentɪd.
22 ɑː θəˈmɒmətə rɪˈkɔːdz ðə ˈtemprɪtʃər ɪn ˈsentɪɡreɪd.
23 ðə kənˈdʌktəz ˈkɒndʌkt wəz ˈkwaɪt ɪmˈprɒpə.
24 ðə mæɡəˈziːn kənˈdʌktɪd ə ˈsɜːveɪ.
25 ˈsevrəl njuː ˈkɒnvɜːts ˈdʒɔɪnd ðə ˈtʃɜːtʃ.

∎

26 ˈhaʊ də jʊ kənˈvɜːt ˈmiːtəz ɪntʊ ˈɪntʃɪz?
27 hɪ wəz ˈduːɪŋ rɪˈsɜːtʃ ɪn ˈretərɪk.
28 əˈrɪθmətɪk ən trɪɡəˈnɒmətrɪ wə hɪz ˈfeɪvərɪt ækəˈdemɪk ˈsʌbdʒekts.
29 ɒn ðə ˈkɒntrərɪ, ˈaɪ faɪnd hə ˈkwaɪt ˈædmərəbl.
30 ˈmeərɪ, ˈmeərɪ, ˈkwaɪt kənˈtreərɪ,
ˈhaʊ dəz jɔː ˈɡɑːdn ˈɡrəʊ?
wɪð ˈsɪlvə ˈbelz ən ˈkɒkl ˈʃelz,
ənd ˈprɪtɪ ˈmeɪdz ˈɔːl ɪn ə ˈrəʊ.

∎

109

PART II
TRANSCRIPTION PRACTICE

34 PROVERBS

- A penny saved is a penny earned.
- His bark is worse than his bite.
- Absence makes the heart grow fonder.
- Blood is thicker than water.
- Brevity is the soul of wit.
- When the cat's away, the mice will play.
- Charity begins at home.
- Every cloud has a silver lining.
- Too many cooks spoil the broth.
- Don't count your chickens before they're hatched.
- One can't have one's cake and eat it too.
- A friend in need is a friend indeed.
- Don't look a gift horse in the mouth.
- All that glitters is not gold.
- Make hay while the sun shines.
- Hunger is the best sauce.
- A Jack of all trades is master of none.
- Better late than never.
- Necessity is the mother of invention.
- A new broom sweeps clean.
- There's no smoke without fire.
- The wish is the father of the thought.
- Two wrongs don't make a right.
- The burnt child dreads fire.
- If the shoe fits, wear it.
- All cats in the dark are grey.
- Don't cross your bridge till you get to it.
- Still waters run deep.
- Easy come, easy go.
- Opposites attract.
- An ounce of prevention is worth a pound of cure.
- No use crying over spilt milk.
- If wishes were horses, beggars would ride.
- Grass is always greener on the other side of the fence.
- The last straw breaks the camel's back.

34 ˈprɒvɜːbz

- ə ˈpenɪ ˈseɪvd ɪz ə ˈpenɪ ˈɜːnd.
- hɪz ˈbɑːk ɪz ˈwɜːs ðən (h)ɪz ˈbaɪt.
- ˈæbs(ə)ns meɪks ðə ˈhɑːt grəʊ ˈfɒndə.
- ˈblʌd ɪz ˈθɪkə ðən ˈwɔːtə.
- ˈbrevətɪ[1] ɪz ðə ˈsəʊl əv ˈwɪt.
- wen ðə ˈkæts əˈweɪ, ðə ˈmaɪs wɪl ˈpleɪ.
- ˈtʃærətɪ[1] bɪˈɡɪnz[2] ət ˈhəʊm.
- ˈevrɪ ˈklaʊd hæz ə ˈsɪlvə ˈlamɪŋ.
- ˈtuː menɪ ˈkʊks ˈspɔɪl ðə ˈbrɒθ.
- ˈdəʊnt ˈkaʊnt jɔː ˈtʃɪkɪnz bɪˈfɔː[2] ðe(ɪ)ə ˈhætʃt.
- wʌn ˈkɑːnt ˈhæv wʌnz ˈkeɪk ən(d) ˈiːt ɪt ˈtuː.
- ə ˈfrend ɪn ˈniːd ɪz ə ˈfrend ɪnˈdiːd.
- ˈdəʊnt lʊk ə ˈɡɪft hɔːs ɪn ðə ˈmaʊθ.
- ˈɔːl ðət ˈɡlɪtəz ɪz nɒt ˈɡəʊld.
- meɪk ˈheɪ waɪl ðə ˈsʌn ˈʃaɪnz.
- ˈhʌŋɡər ɪz ðə ˈbest ˈsɔːs.
- ə ˈdʒæk əv ɔːl ˈtreɪdz ɪz ˈmɑːstər əv ˈnʌn.
- ˈbetə ˈleɪt ðən ˈnevə.
- nɪˈsesətɪ[3/1] ɪz ðə ˈmʌðər əv ɪnˈvenʃn.
- ə ˈnjuː ˈbruːm[4] swiːps ˈkliːn.
- ðəz ˈnəʊ ˈsməʊk wɪðaʊt ˈfaɪə.
- ðə ˈwɪʃ ɪz ðə ˈfɑːðər əv ðə ˈθɔːt.
- ˈtuː ˈrɒŋz ˈdəʊnt meɪk ə ˈraɪt.
- ðə ˈbɜːnt ˈtʃaɪld dredz ˈfaɪə.
- ɪf ðə ˈʃuː ˈfɪts, ˈweər ɪt.
- ˈɔːl ˈkæts ɪn ðə ˈdɑːk ə ˈɡreɪ.
- ˈdəʊnt ˈkrɒs jɔː ˈbrɪdʒ tɪl jʊ ˈɡet tʊ[5] ɪt.
- ˈstɪl ˈwɔːtəz rʌn ˈdiːp.
- iːzɪ ˈkʌm, iːzɪ ˈɡəʊ.
- ˈɒpəzɪts[6] əˈtrækt.
- ən ˈaʊns əv prɪˈvenʃn[7] ɪz wɜːθ ə ˈpaʊnd əv ˈkjʊə.
- nəʊ juːs ˈkraɪɪŋ əʊvə ˈspɪlt ˈmɪlk.
- ɪf ˈwɪʃɪz wə ˈhɔːsɪz, ˈbeɡəz wəd[8] ˈraɪd.
- ˈɡrɑːs ɪz ɔːlw(e)ɪz[9] ˈɡriːnər ɒn ðɪ ˈʌðə saɪd əv ðə ˈfens.
- ðə ˈlɑːst ˈstrɔː breɪks ðə ˈkæmlz ˈbæk.

---

[1] -ɪtɪ [2] bə- [3] nə-, ne- [4] brʊm [5] tuː [6] -əsɪts [7] prə- [8] wʊd [9] -wəz

35 PHONETIC CROSSWORD PUZZLE

Transcribe the following words into the puzzle:

ACROSS

1 great
5 slimly
11 rule
12 retinues
14 included
16 ooze
17 ethic
18 as
20 effete
23 in
25 imp
27 ears
28 egg
30 off course
32 ill
34 revolt
37 Oedipus
38 ad
40 bless
42 Mel
43 Ely
44 lightweight
46 zip
47 Ike
48 Acis
50 Icarus
51 zooming

DOWN

1 grenade
2 rune
3 elk
4 truth
5 sticky
6 lid
7 inn
8 musical
9 lose
10 is
13 eddy
15 let
19 apse
21 for (WF)
22 easy
24 novelties
26 mortality
29 grimace
31 fosse
33 leased
35 apace
36 alike
39 dip
40 Bligh
41 acre
43 ease
45 wear
49 Sioux

36

Sing a song of sixpence, a pocket full of rye;
Four and twenty blackbirds, baked in a pie.

When the pie was opened, the birds began to sing;
Wasn't that a dainty dish, to set before a king?

The king was in his counting-house, counting out his money;
The queen was in the parlour, eating bread and honey.

The maid was in the garden, hanging out the clothes,
There came a little blackbird, and snapped off her nose.

36

ˈsɪŋ ə ˈsɒŋ əv ˈsɪkspəns, ə ˈpɒkɪt ˈfʊl əv ˈraɪ;
ˈfɔːr ən(d) ˈtwentɪ ˈblækbɜːdz, ˈbeɪkt ˈɪn ə ˈpaɪ.
ˈwen ðə ˈpaɪ wəz ˈəʊp(ə)nd, ðə ˈbɜːdz bɪˈgæn[1] tə ˈsɪŋ;
ˈwɒznt ðæt ə ˈdeɪntɪ ˈdɪʃ, tə ˈset bɪˈfɔːr[1] ə ˈkɪŋ?

ðə ˈkɪŋ wəz ˈɪn (h)ɪz ˈkaʊntɪŋ haʊs, ˈkaʊntɪŋ ˈaʊt (h)ɪz ˈmʌnɪ;
ðə ˈkwiːn wəz ˈɪn ðə ˈpɑːlə, ˈiːtɪŋ ˈbred ən(d) ˈhʌnɪ.
ðə ˈmeɪd wəz ˈɪn ðə ˈgɑːdn, ˈhæŋɪŋ ˈaʊt ðə ˈkləʊ(ð)z,
ðeə ˈkeɪm ə ˈlɪtl ˈblækbɜːd, ən(d) ˈsnæpt ˈɒf (h)ə ˈnəʊz.

---

[1] bə-

37 TOM THUMB'S ALPHABET

A was an Archer, who shot at a frog;
B was a Butcher, who had a great dog;
C was a Captain, all covered with lace;
D was a Drunkard, and had a red face;
E was an Esquire, with pride on his brow;
F was a Farmer, and followed the plough;
G was a Gamester, who had but ill luck;
H was a Hunter, who hunted a buck;
I was an Innkeeper, who loved to carouse;
J was a Joiner, who built up a house;
K was a King, so mighty and grand;
L was a Lady, who had a white hand;
M was a Miser, and hoarded up gold;
N was a Nobleman, gallant and bold;
O was an Oysterman, who went about town;
P was a Parson, and wore a black gown;
Q was a Quack, with a wonderful pill;
R was a Robber, who wanted to kill;
S was a Sailor, who spent all he got;
T was a Tinker, and mended a pot;
U was a Usurer, a miserable elf;
V was a Vintner, who drank all himself;
W was a Watchman, who guarded the door;
X was Expensive, and so became poor;
Y was a Youth, that did not love school;
Z was a Zany, a poor harmless fool.

38

The easiest way to give the impression of having a good accent or no foreign accent at all is to hold an unlit pipe in your mouth, to mutter between your teeth and finish all your sentences with the question 'isn't it'. People will not understand much, but they are accustomed to that and they will get a most excellent impression.

Georges Mikes, *How to be an Alien*

37 ˈtɒm ˈθʌmz ˈælfəbɪt[1]

ˈeɪ wəz ən ˈɑːtʃə, hʊ ˈʃɒt ət ə ˈfrɒɡ;
ˈbiː wəz ə ˈbʊtʃə, hʊ ˈhæd ə ɡreɪt ˈdɒɡ;
ˈsiː wəz ə ˈkæptɪn, ɔːl ˈkʌvəd wɪð ˈleɪs;
ˈdiː wəz ə ˈdrʌŋkəd, ən(d) ˈhæd ə red ˈfeɪs;
ˈiː wəz ən ˈeskwaɪə, wɪð ˈpraɪd ɒn (h)ɪz ˈbraʊ;
ˈef wəz ə ˈfɑːmə, ən(d) ˈfɒləʊd ðə ˈplaʊ;
ˈdʒiː wəz ə ˈɡeɪmstə, hʊ ˈhæd bət ɪl ˈlʌk;
ˈeɪtʃ wəz ə ˈhʌntə, hʊ ˈhʌntɪd ə ˈbʌk;
ˈaɪ wəz ən ˈɪŋkiːpə, hʊ ˈlʌvd tə kəˈraʊz;
ˈdʒeɪ wəz ə ˈdʒɔɪnə, hʊ ˈbɪlt ʌp ə ˈhaʊs;
ˈkeɪ wəz ə ˈkɪŋ, səʊ ˈmaɪtɪ ən(d) ˈɡrænd;
ˈel wəz ə ˈleɪdɪ, hʊ ˈhæd ə waɪt ˈhænd;
ˈem wəz ə ˈmaɪzə, ən(d) ˈhɔːdɪd ʌp ˈɡəʊld;
ˈen wəz ə ˈnəʊblmən, ˈɡælənt ən(d) ˈbəʊld;
ˈəʊ wəz ən ˈɔɪstəmən, hʊ ˈwent əbaʊt ˈtaʊn;
ˈpiː wəz ə ˈpɑːsn, ən(d) ˈwɔːr ə blæk ˈɡaʊn;
ˈkjuː wəz ə ˈkwæk, wɪð ə ˈwʌndəf(ʊ)l ˈpɪl;
ˈɑː wəz ə ˈrɒbə, hʊ ˈwɒntɪd tə ˈkɪl;
ˈes wəz ə ˈseɪlə, hʊ ˈspent ɔːl (h)ɪ ˈɡɒt;
ˈtiː wəz ə ˈtɪŋkə, ən(d) ˈmendɪd ə ˈpɒt;
ˈjuː wəz ə ˈjuːʒ(ə)rə, ə ˈmɪz(ə)r(ə)bl ˈelf;
ˈviː wəz ə ˈvɪntnə, hʊ ˈdræŋk ɔːl (h)ɪmˈself;
ˈdʌbljuː wəz ə ˈwɒtʃmən, hʊ ˈɡɑːdɪd ðə ˈdɔː;
ˈeks wəz ɪkˈspensɪv[2], ən(d) ˈsəʊ bɪkeɪm[3] ˈpɔː;
ˈwaɪ wəz ə ˈjuːθ, ðət ˈdɪdnt lʌv ˈskuːl;
ˈzed wəz ə ˈzeɪnɪ, ə ˈpʊə[4] hɑːmlɪs[5] ˈfuːl.

---

[1] -bet [2] eks- [3] bə- [4] pɔː [5] -ləs

38

ðɪ ˈiːzɪɪst[1] ˈweɪ tə ɡɪv ðɪ ɪmˈpreʃn əv ˈhævɪŋ ə ˈɡʊd ˈæks(ə)nt[2] ɔː ˈnəʊ ˈfɒrɪn[3] ˈæks(ə)nt[2] ət ˈɔːl ɪz tə ˈhəʊld ən ˈʌnlɪt ˈpaɪp ɪn jɔː ˈmaʊθ, tə ˈmʌtə brɪˈtwiːn[4] jɔː ˈtiːθ ən(d) ˈfɪnɪʃ ˈɔːl jɔː ˈsentənsɪz wɪð ðə ˈkwestʃn ˈɪznt ɪt. ˈpiːpl wɪl ˈnɒt ʌndəˈstænd ˈmʌtʃ, bət ðe(ɪ)r əˈkʌstəmd tə ˈðæt ən(d) ðeɪ wɪl ˈɡet ə ˈməʊst ˈeksələnt ɪmˈpreʃn.

---

[1] -jɪst [2] -ent [3] -ən [4] bə-

39 PHONETIC CROSSWORD PUZZLE

Transcribe the following words into the puzzle:

ACROSS

1 supersede
7 date
10 ecology
12 spring
13 mated
15 in
16 certain
17 am (WF)
18 mill
20 Faraday
21 in
22 Bali
23 ad
24 stay
26 ingot
29 Turk
30 Anne
31 orison
33 sand
34 belly
35 eat
37 jelly
38 thee
40 tundra
42 ill
43 as (WF)
44 bee
45 on
46 easy

DOWN

1 Sesame Street
2 peril
3 akin
4 song
5 eal
6 demurring
7 ginger ale
8 eight
9 Todmorden
11 debtor
14 ear
16 Salinger
19 inter (v.)
20 far
22 be (WF)
25 ex
27 goblin
28 till
30 Andrew
32 zithers
36 tub
39 easy
41 knee

40

Among the attractions of Anglesey, an island off the coast of North Wales, is a village which can boast no less than fifty-eight letters in its name: Llanfairpwllgwyngyllgogerychwyrndrobwllllantysiliogogogoch. What a jawbreaker!

A traveller returning from Wales reports that whenever a train stops at this place, the conductor simply calls out: "If anybody's getting out here, this is it."

For obvious reasons this Welsh place name has been abbreviated to Llanfair P.G.

40

əmʌŋ ði əˈtrækʃnz əv ˈæŋglsɪ, ən ˈaɪlənd ˈɒf ðə ˈkəʊst əv ˈnɔːθ ˈweɪlz ɪz ə ˈvɪlɪdʒ wɪtʃ kən bəʊst ˈnəʊ ˈles ðən ˈfɪftɪ ˈeɪt ˈletəz ɪn ɪts ˈneɪm: ˌlanvair-puɬgwingɨlgogerɨxwɨrndrobuɬɬantɨsiliogogogox. ˈwɒt ə ˈdʒɔːbreɪkə!

ə ˈtrævlə rɪˈtɜːnɪŋ[1] frəm ˈweɪlz rɪˈpɔːts[1] ðət wenˈevər ə ˈtreɪn ˈstɒps ət ðɪs ˈpleɪs, ðə kənˈdʌktə ˈsɪmplɪ ˈkɔːlz ˈaʊt: ɪf ˈenɪbɒdɪz[2] ˈgetɪŋ ˈaʊt ˈhɪə, ˈðɪs ɪz ˈɪt.

fər ˈɒbvɪəs ˈriːznz ˈðɪs ˈwelʃ ˈpleɪs neɪm (h)əz bɪn əˈbriːvɪeɪtɪd[3] tə ˈlanvair ˈpiː ˈdʒiː[4].

---

[1] rə-   [2] -bədɪz   [3] -vjeɪt-   [4] Non-Welsh speakers would usually pronounce this place name – given above in its Welsh phonetic transcription – as follows: (θ)lænfeə, -vaɪə

119

41 A BRICKLAYER'S STORY

When I got to the top of the building, I found that the hurricane had knocked some bricks off the top. So I rigged up a beam with a pulley at the top of the building and hoisted up a couple of barrels full of bricks. When I had fixed the building, there was a lot of bricks left over. I hoisted the barrel back up again and secured the line at the bottom, and then went up and filled the barrel with extra bricks. Then I went to the bottom and cast off the line. Unfortunately, the barrel of bricks was heavier than I was, and before I knew what was happening, the barrel started down, jerking me off the ground. I decided to hang on, and halfway up I met the barrel coming down, and received a severe blow on the shoulder. I then continued to the top, banging my head against the beam and getting my fingers jammed in the pulley. When the barrel hit the ground, it burst at its bottom, allowing all the bricks to spill out. I was now heavier than the barrel, and so started down again at high speed. Halfway down, I met the barrel coming up, and received severe injury to my shins. When I hit the ground, I landed on the bricks, getting several painful cuts from the sharp edges. At this point I must have lost my presence of mind, because I let go the line. The barrel then came down, giving me another heavy blow and putting me in hospital.

42

A dog-loving doctor had the habit of training his Alsatian puppy in his garden during the early hours of the morning. One Sunday a neighbour was so annoyed at being woken by the doctor's loud commands "heel, heel" that he opened the window and shouted angrily over the fence: "Physician, heal thyself".

43

Smythe: I'll be a grass widower for the next two months.
My wife's going for a holiday to the West Indies.
Callaghan: Jamaica?
Smythe: No, it was her own idea.

41 ə ˈbrɪkle(ɪ)əz ˈstɔːrɪ

wen aɪ ˈɡɒt tə ðə ˈtɒp əv ðə ˈbɪldɪŋ, aɪ ˈfaʊnd ðət ðə ˈhʌrɪkən[1] (h)əd ˈnɒkt səm ˈbrɪks ˈɒf ðə ˈtɒp. səʊ aɪ ˈrɪɡd ˈʌp ə ˈbiːm wɪð ə ˈpʊlɪ ət ðə ˈtɒp əv ðə ˈbɪldɪŋ ən(d) ˈhɔɪstɪd ˈʌp ə ˈkʌpl əv ˈbær(ə)lz ˈfʊl əv ˈbrɪks. wen aɪ (h)(ə)d ˈfɪkst ðə ˈbɪldɪŋ, ðə wəz ə ˈlɒt əv ˈbrɪks left ˈəʊvə. aɪ ˈhɔɪstɪd ðə ˈbær(ə)l ˈbæk ˈʌp əˈɡe(ɪ)n ən(d) sɪˈkjʊəd[2] ðə ˈlaɪn ət ðə ˈbɒtəm, ən(d) ˈðen ˈwent ˈʌp ən(d) ˈfɪld ðə ˈbær(ə)l wɪð ˈekstrə ˈbrɪks. ˈðen aɪ ˈwent tə ðə ˈbɒtəm ən(d) ˈkɑːst ˈɒf ðə ˈlaɪn. ʌnˈfɔːtʃ(ə)nətlɪ[3], ðə ˈbær(ə)l əv ˈbrɪks wəz ˈhevɪə[4] ðən ˈaɪ ˈwɒz, ən(d) bɪˈfɔːr[5] aɪ ˈnjuː: wɒt wəz ˈhæp(ə)nɪŋ ðə ˈbær(ə)l ˈstɑːtɪd ˈdaʊn, ˈdʒɜːkɪŋ mɪ ˈɒf ðə ˈɡraʊnd. aɪ dɪˈsaɪdɪd tə ˈhæŋ ˈɒn, ən(d) ˈhɑːfweɪ ˈʌp aɪ ˈmet ðə ˈbær(ə)l ˈkʌmɪŋ ˈdaʊn, ən(d) rɪˈsiːvd[6] ə sɪˈvɪə[7] ˈbləʊ ɒn ðɔ ʃəʊldə. aɪ ˈðen kənˈtɪnjuːd tə ðə ˈtɒp, ˈbæŋɪŋ maɪ ˈhed əɡe(ɪ)nst ðə ˈbiːm ən(d) ˈɡetɪŋ maɪ ˈfɪŋɡəz ˈdʒæmd ɪn ðə ˈpʊlɪ. wen ðə ˈbær(ə)l ˈhɪt ðə ˈɡraʊnd, ɪt ˈbɜːst ət ɪts ˈbɒtəm, əˈlaʊɪŋ ˈɔːl ðə ˈbrɪks tə ˈspɪl ˈaʊt. ˈaɪ wəz ˈnaʊ ˈhevɪə[4] ðən ðə ˈbær(ə)l, ən(d) ˈsəʊ ˈstɑːtɪd ˈdaʊn əˈɡe(ɪ)n ət ˈhaɪ ˈspiːd. ˈhɑːfweɪ daʊn, aɪ ˈmet ðə ˈbær(ə)l ˈkʌmɪŋ ˈʌp, ən(d) rɪˈsiːvd[6] sɪˈvɪər[7] ˈɪndʒərɪ tə maɪ ˈʃɪnz. wen aɪ ˈhɪt ðə ˈɡraʊnd, aɪ ˈlændɪd ɒn ðə ˈbrɪks, ˈɡetɪŋ ˈsevr(ə)l ˈpeɪnf(ʊ)l ˈkʌts frəm ðə ˈʃɑːp ˈedʒɪz. ət ˈðɪs ˈpɔɪnt aɪ ˈmʌst (h)əv ˈlɒst maɪ ˈprezns əv ˈmaɪnd, bɪkɒz[5/8] aɪ ˈlet ˈɡəʊ ðə ˈlaɪn. ðə ˈbær(ə)l ˈðen keɪm ˈdaʊn, ˈɡɪvɪŋ mɪ əˈnʌðə ˈhevɪ ˈbləʊ ən(d) ˈpʊtɪŋ mɪ ɪn ˈhɒspɪtl.

---

[1] k(e)ɪn [2] sə-, -kjɔːd [3] -ɪtlɪ [4] -jə [5] bə- [6] rə- [7] sə- [8] bɪkəz

42

ə ˈdɒɡ lʌvɪŋ ˈdɒktə hæd ðə ˈhæbɪt əv ˈtreɪnɪŋ (h)ɪz ælˈseɪʃ(ə)n[1] ˈpʌpɪ ɪn (h)ɪz ˈɡɑːdn djʊərɪŋ[2] ðɪ ˈɜːlɪ ˈaʊəz əv ðə ˈmɔːnɪŋ. ˈwʌn ˈsʌndɪ[3] ə ˈneɪbə wəz ˈsəʊ əˈnɔɪd ət biːɪŋ ˈwəʊk(ə)n baɪ ðə ˈdɒktəz ˈlaʊd kəˈmɑːndz ˈhiːl, ˈhiːl ðət (h)ɪ ˈəʊp(ə)nd ðə ˈwɪndəʊ ən(d) ˈʃaʊtɪd ˈæŋɡrəlɪ[4] əʊvə ðə ˈfens: fɪˈzɪʃn, ˈhiːl ðɑːˈself.

---

[1] -ʃ(ɪə)n [2] dʒʊə-, djɔː-, dʒɔː- [3] -deɪ [4] -ɪlɪ

43

ˈsmaɪð[1]: aɪl bɪ ə ˈɡrɑːs ˈwɪdəʊə fə ðə ˈneks(t) tuː: ˈmʌn(θ)s.
maɪ ˈwaɪfs ˈɡəʊɪŋ fər ə ˈhɒlədɪ[2] tə ðə ˈwest ˈɪndɪz.
ˈkæləhən: dʒəˈmeɪkə?
smaɪð[1]: ˈnəʊ, ɪt wəz (h)ər ˈəʊn aɪˈdɪə.

---

[1] -θ [2] -lɪ-, -deɪ

44 PHONETIC WORD PUZZLE: BRITISH AUTHORS

A transcription of each of the listed words is to be found within the puzzle diagram. Words can be found reading UP, DOWN, FORWARDS, BACKWARDS and DIAGONALLY throughout the puzzle. Words can overlap each other and letters can be used more than once. Words always run in a straight line and never skip any letters. Once you have found a word in the diagram, circle it and cross it off the word list. The puzzle is complete once all words have been located in the diagram.

After completing the entire puzzle you are left with *5 symbols*. Juggle them around and you will come up with an additional English author.

Bede	Dickens	More	Thackeray
Boyle	Donne		Trollope
Buchanan	Dryden	Pepys	
Bunyan		Peele	Wesley
Burns	Fielding	Percy	Wilde
		Porter	Wordsworth
Chaucer	Hardy		Wycherley
Cooper	Hazlitt	Raleigh	Wyclif
Crabbe	Hood	Rossetti	
Cromwell	Hunt		Yeats
		Shakespeare	
Darwin	Keats	Shelley	

45 THE PRODIGAL SON

'There was once a man who had two sons; and the younger said to his father, "Father, give me my share of the property." So he divided his estate between them. A few days later the younger son turned the whole of his share into cash and left home for a distant country, where he squandered it in reckless living. He had spent it all, when a severe famine fell upon that country and he began to feel the pinch. So he went and attached himself to one of the local landowners, who sent him on to his farm to mind the pigs. He would have been glad to fill his belly with the pods that the pigs were eating; and no one gave him anything. Then he came to his senses and said, "How many of my father's paid servants have more food than they can eat, and here am I, starving to death! I will set off and go to my father, and say to him, 'Father, I have sinned,

b	d	b	w	e	s	l	ɪ	s	ɜː	p	ɪ
ɜː	ʊ	ʌ	ɪ	w	ɜː	d	z	w	ə	θ	t
n	h	n	k	l	ɑː	ɪ	t	e	s	ɒ	r
z	æ	j	l	w	ə	ə	p	uː	k	ɔː	ɒ
n	z	ə	ɪ	m	ɪ	ʃ	ɔː	s	l	m	l
ə	l	n	f	ɔː	p	s	t	ɪ	e	j	ə
n	ɪ	n	ɪ	s	s	iː	ə	ɪ	l	iː	p
æ	t	ɪ	p	k	k	r	ɒ	m	w	ə	l
k	f	iː	l	d	ɪ	ŋ	k	l	a	l	t
uː	p	d	t	e	e	d	r	a	ɪ	d	n
j	iː	ə	s	ɔː	ʃ	t	æ	ɔ	l	ʌ	ʌ
b	θ	æ	k	ə	r	ɪ	b	ɪ	d	ɑː	h

45 ðə ˈprɒdɪgl ˈsʌn

ðə wəz ˈwʌns ə ˈmæn hu hæd ˈtuː ˈsʌnz; ən(d) ðə ˈjʌŋgə ˈsed tə hɪz[1] ˈfɑːðə, ˈfɑːðə, ˈgɪv mɪ ˈmaɪ ˈʃeər əv ðə ˈprɒpətɪ. ˈsəʊ (h)ɪ dɪˈvaɪdɪd (h)ɪz ɪˈsteɪt brɪˈtwiːn[2] ðəm. ə ˈfjuː deɪz ˈleɪtə ðə ˈjʌŋgə ˈsʌn ˈtɜːnd ðə ˈhəʊl əv (h)ɪz ˈʃeər ɪntə ˈkæʃ ən(d) ˈleft ˈhəʊm fər ə ˈdɪst(ə)nt ˈkʌntrɪ, weə hɪ[3] ˈskwɒndəd ɪt ɪn ˈreklɪs[4] ˈlɪvɪŋ. hɪ (h)əd[5] ˈspent ɪt ˈɔːl, wen ə sɪˈvɪə[6] ˈfæmɪn ˈfel əpɒn[7] ðæt ˈkʌntrɪ ən(d) (h)ɪ brɪˈgæn[2] tə ˈfiːl ðə ˈpɪn(t)ʃ. ˈsəʊ (h)ɪ ˈwent ən(d) əˈtætʃt (h)ɪmself tʊ ˈwʌn əv ðə ˈləʊkl ˈlændəʊnəz, hu ˈsent (h)ɪm ˈɒn tə hɪz[1] ˈfɑːm tə ˈmaɪnd ðə ˈpɪgz. hɪ wəd (h)əv bɪn ˈglæd tə ˈfɪl (h)ɪ ˈbelɪ wɪð ðə ˈpɒdz ðət ðə ˈpɪgz wər iːtɪŋ; ən(d) ˈnəʊ wʌn ˈgeɪv (h)ɪm ˈenɪθɪŋ. ˈðen (h)ɪ ˈkeɪm tə hɪz[1] ˈsensɪz ən(d) ˈsed, ˈhaʊ ˈmenɪ əv maɪ ˈfɑːðəz ˈpeɪd ˈsɜːv(ə)nts hæv ˈmɔː ˈfuːd ðən ðeɪ kən ˈiːt, ən(d) ˈhɪər əm ˈaɪ, ˈstɑːvɪŋ tə ˈdeθ. ˈaɪ (w)(ə)l ˈset ˈɒf ən(d) ˈgəʊ tə maɪ ˈfɑːðə, ən(d) ˈseɪ tə hɪm[8], ˈfɑːðə, aɪ (h)(ə)v ˈsɪnd, əge(ɪ)nst gɒd ən(d) əge(ɪ)nst ˈjuː. aɪ (ə)m ˈnəʊ

---

[1] tʊ ɪz [2] bə- [3] weər ɪ [4] -ləs [5] hiːd [6] sə- [7] əpən [8] tʊ ɪm

against God and against you; I am no longer fit to be called your son; treat me as one of your paid servants.'" So he set out for his father's house. But while he was still a long way off his father saw him, and his heart went out to him. He ran to meet him, flung his arms round him, and kissed him. The son said, "Father, I have sinned, against God and against you; I am no longer fit to be called your son." But the father said to his servants, "Quick! fetch a robe, my best one, and put it on him; put a ring on his finger and shoes on his feet. Bring the fatted calf and kill it, and let us have a feast to celebrate the day. For this son of mine was dead and has come back to life; he was lost and is found." And the festivities began.'

New English Bible

46 /s/ AND /z/ WORD PUZZLE

(For directions see p. 122)

After completing the puzzle you will be left with 5 /s/ and 6 /z/.

absolve	infuse	scissors
advice	inns	sears
arouse	is	seesaw
ass	lice (2x)	Sue
assault	lizard	Sioux (pl.)
	loose	Swansea
cease		
close (adj.)	Missouri	
course	Miss	tease
crease	Mrs.	tense
	More's	tinsel
desert (2x)		tons
disease	nose	twos
dose		
	pansy	use (v.)
his	precious	
house (n.)	purse	vice
houses		
	reads	Zulu

lɒŋɡə 'fɪt tə bɪ 'kɔːld jɔː 'sʌn. 'triːt mɪ əz 'wʌn əv jɔː 'peɪd 'sɜːv(ə)nts. 'səʊ (h)ɪ 'set 'aʊt fə hɪz⁹ 'fɑːðəz 'haʊs. bət 'waɪl (h)ɪ wəz 'stɪl ə 'lɒŋ weɪ 'ɒf hɪz 'fɑːðə 'sɔː (h)ɪm, ən(d) (h)ɪz 'hɑːt went 'aʊt tə hɪm⁸. hɪ 'ræn tə 'miːt (h)ɪm, 'flʌŋ (h)ɪz 'ɑːmz raʊnd (h)ɪm, ən(d) 'kɪst (h)ɪm. ðə 'sʌn 'sed, 'fɑːðə, aɪ (h)(ə)v 'sɪnd, əɡe(ɪ)nst 'ɡɒd ənd əɡe(ɪ)nst 'juː; aɪ (ə)m 'nəʊ lɒŋɡə 'fɪt tə bɪ 'kɔːld jɔː 'sʌn. bət ðə 'fɑːðə 'sed tə hɪz¹ 'sɜːv(ə)nts, 'kwɪk! 'fetʃ ə 'rəʊb, maɪ 'best wʌn, ən(d) 'pʊt ɪt 'ɒn (h)ɪm; 'pʊt ə 'rɪŋ ɒn (h)ɪz 'fɪŋɡər ən(d) 'ʃuːz ɒn (h)ɪz 'fiːt. 'brɪŋ ðə 'fætɪd 'kɑːf ən(d) 'kɪl ɪt, ən(d) 'let (ə)s 'hæv ə 'fiːst tə 'selɪbreɪt ðə 'deɪ. fə 'ðɪs 'sʌn əv 'maɪn wəz 'ded ən(d) (h)əz 'kʌm 'bæk tə 'laɪf; hɪ wəz 'lɒst ən(d) ɪz 'faʊnd. ən(d) ðə feˈstɪvətɪz¹⁰ bɪˈɡæn².

⁹ fər ɪz   ¹⁰ -ɪtɪz

46

z	s	z	s	z	s	z	s	z	s	z	s
z	ʊ	a	r	ə	uː	ɪ	p	æ	n	z	ɪ
h	ə	iː	ʃ	l	a	j	z	ɪ	s	ɪ	m
ɪ	d	e	uː	v	v	l	ɒ	z	b	ə	k
z	r	s	d	l	a	ɪ	s	ɪ	a	l	ɔː
p	ɪ	ə	s	d	ɪ	z	iː	z	ə	ɪ	s
ɜː	z	n	ʊ	e	s	ə	s	ʊ	a	h	ɪ
s	ɪ	t	ə	z	e	d	s	a	z	n	z
t	l	ɔː	s	ə	ɪ	k	s	h	f	ə	n
ʌ	e	z	s	t	r	m	uː	j	z	ə	ɒ
n	s	n	uː	iː	ɔː	æ	uː	ɪ	ʊ	uː	w
z	s	z	s	z	s	z	s	z	s	z	s

LIZA [*desperate*]

I'll marry Freddy, I will, as soon as I'm able to support him.

HIGGINS [*thunderstruck*] Freddy!!! that young fool! That poor devil who couldnt get a job as an errand boy even if he had the guts to try for it! Woman: do you not understand that I have made you a consort for a king?

LIZA. Freddy loves me: that makes him king enough for me. I dont want him to work: he wasnt brought up to it as I was. I'll go and be a teacher.

HIGGINS. Whatll you teach, in heaven's name?

LIZA. What you taught me. I'll teach phonetics.

HIGGINS. Ha! ha! ha!

LIZA. I'll offer myself as an assistant to that hairyfaced Hungarian.

HIGGINS [*rising in a fury*] What! That impostor! that humbug! that toadying ignoramus! Teach him my methods! my discoveries! You take one step in his direction and I'll wring your neck. [*He lays hands on her*]. Do you hear?

LIZA [*defiantly non-resistant*] Wring away. What do I care? I knew youd strike me some day. [*He lets her go, stamping with rage at having forgotten himself, and recoils so hastily that he stumbles back into his seat on the ottoman*]. Aha! Now I know how to deal with you. What a fool I was not to think of it before! You cant take away the knowledge you gave me. You said I had a finer ear than you. And I can be civil and kind to people, which is more than you can. Aha! [*Purposely dropping her aitches to annoy him*] Thats done you, Enry Iggins, it az. Now I dont care that [*snapping her fingers*] for your bullying and your big talk. I'll advertize it in the papers that your duchess is only a flower girl that you taught, and that she'll teach anybody to be a duchess just the same in six months for a thousand guineas. Oh, when I think of myself crawling under your feet and being trampled on and called names, when all the time I had only to lift up my finger to be as good as you, I could just kick myself.

HIGGINS [*wondering at her*] You damned impudent slut, you! But it's better than snivelling; better than fetching slippers and finding spectacles, isnt it? [*Rising*] By George, Eliza, I said I'd make a woman of you; and I have. I like you like this.

Bernard Shaw, *Pygmalion*

ˈlaɪzə (desp(ə)rət¹)
aɪl ˈmærɪ ˈfredɪ, aɪ ˈwɪl, əz ˈsuːn əz aɪm ˈeɪbl tə səˈpɔːt (h)ɪm.

ˈhɪgɪnz (ˈθʌndəstrʌk) ˈfredɪ!!! ðæt jʌŋ ˈfuːl! ðæt ˈpʊə² ˈdevl hʊ ˈkʊdn(t) get ə ˈdʒɒb əz ən ˈerən(d) bɔɪ ˈiːvn ɪf (h)ɪ hæd ðə ˈɡʌts tə traɪ fər³ ɪt! ˈwʊmən: dʊ⁴ jʊ ˈnɒt ʌndəˈstænd ðət aɪv ˈmeɪd jʊ ə ˈkɒnsɔːt fər ə ˈkɪŋ?

ˈlaɪzə: ˈfredɪ ˈlʌvz mɪ: ðæt meɪks (h)ɪm ˈkɪŋ ɪˈnʌf⁵ fə ˈmiː. aɪ dəʊnt ˈwɒnt (h)ɪm tʊ ˈwɜːk: hɪ ˈwɒznt brɔːt ˈʌp tʊ ɪt əz ˈaɪ ˈwɒz. aɪl ˈɡəʊ ən(d) bɪ ə ˈtiːtʃə.

ˈhɪgɪnz: ˈwɒtl jʊ ˈtiːtʃ, ɪn ˈhevnz ˈneɪm?

ˈlaɪzə: wɒt ˈjuː ˈtɔːt mɪ. aɪl ˈtiːtʃ fəˈ(ʊ)ˈnetɪks.

ˈhɪgɪnz: ˈhɑː! ˈhɑː! ˈhɑː!

ˈlaɪzə: aɪl ˈɒfə maɪself əz ən əˈsɪst(ə)nt tə ðæt ˈheərɪfeɪst hʌŋˈɡeərɪən.

ˈhɪgɪnz (ˈraɪzɪŋ ɪn ə ˈfjʊərɪⁿ) wɒt! ðæt ɪmˈpɒstə! ðæt ˈhʌmbʌɡ! ðæt ˈtəʊdiɪŋ⁷ ɪɡnəˈreɪməs⁸! ˈtiːtʃ (h)ɪm ˈmaɪ ˈmeθədz! maɪ dɪˈskʌv(ə)rɪz! ˈjuː teɪk ˈwʌn ˈstep ɪn ˈhɪz dɪˈrekʃn⁹ ən(d) aɪl ˈrɪŋ jɔː ˈnek. (hɪ leɪz ˈhændz ɒn (h)ə). dʊ⁴ jʊ ˈhɪə?

ˈlaɪzə (dɪˈfaɪəntlɪ ˈnɒn-rɪˈzɪst(ə)nt¹⁰) ˈrɪŋ əˈweɪ. wɒt dʊ ˈaɪ ˈkeə? aɪ ˈnjuː juːd ˈstraɪk mɪ ˈsʌm ˈdeɪ. (hɪ ˈlets (h)ə ˈɡəʊ, ˈstæmpɪŋ wɪð ˈreɪdʒ ət hævɪŋ fəˈɡɒtn (h)ɪmˈself, ən(d) rɪˈkɔɪlz¹⁰ səʊ ˈheɪstɪlɪ¹¹ ðət (h)ɪ ˈstʌmblz ˈbæk ɪntə¹² hɪz ˈsiːt ɒn ðɪ ˈɒtə(ʊ)mən). ɑːˈhɑː:¹³. naʊ aɪ ˈnəʊ haʊ tə ˈdiːl wɪð ˈjuː. wɒt ə ˈfuːl aɪ ˈwɒz ˈnɒt tə ˈθɪŋk əv ɪt bɪˈfɔː:!¹⁴ jʊ ˈkɑːnt teɪk əˈweɪ ðə ˈnɒlɪdʒ jʊ ˈɡeɪv mɪ. jʊ ˈsed ˈaɪ hæd ə ˈfaɪnər ˈɪə ðən ˈjuː. ən(d) ˈaɪ kən bɪ ˈsɪv(ɪ)l ən(d) ˈkaɪnd tə ˈpiːpl, wɪtʃ ɪz ˈmɔː: ðən ˈjuː: ˈkæn. ɑːˈhɑː:! (ˈpɜːpəslɪ ˈdrɒpɪŋ (h)ər ˈeɪtʃɪz tʊ əˈnɔɪ (h)ɪm). ðæts ˈdʌn ˈjuː:, ˈenrɪ ˈɪɡɪnz, ɪt ˈæz. naʊ aɪ dəʊn(t) keə ˈðæt (ˈsnæpɪŋ (h)ə ˈfɪŋɡəz) fə jɔː: ˈbʊlɪɪŋ ən(d) jɔː: ˈbɪɡ tɔːk. aɪl ˈædvətaɪz ɪt ɪn ðə ˈpeɪpəz ðət jɔː: ˈdʌtʃɪs¹⁵ ɪz ˈəʊnlɪ ə ˈflaʊə ɡɜːl ðət jʊ ˈtɔːt, ən(d) ðət ʃiːl ˈtiːtʃ ˈenɪbɒdɪ¹⁶ tə bɪ ə ˈdʌtʃɪs¹⁵ ˈdʒʌs(t) ðə ˈseɪm ɪn ˈsɪks ˈmʌn(θ)s fər ə ˈθaʊznd ˈɡɪnɪz. ˈəʊ wen aɪ ˈθɪŋk əv maɪˈself ˈkrɔːlɪŋ ʌndə jɔː: ˈfiːt ən(d) biːɪŋ ˈtræmpld ˈɒn ən(d) ˈkɔːld ˈneɪmz, wen ˈɔːl ðə ˈtaɪm aɪ hæd ˈəʊnlɪ tə ˈlɪft ˈʌp maɪ ˈfɪŋɡə tə bɪ əz ˈɡʊd əz ˈjuː:, aɪ kəd ˈdʒʌs(t) ˈkɪk maɪˈself.

ˈhɪgɪnz, (ˈwʌnd(ə)rɪŋ ət (h)ə) ˈjuː: ˈdæmd ɪmˈpjʊd(ə)nt ˈslʌt, ˈjuː:! bət ɪts ˈbetə ðən ˈsnɪvlɪŋ; ˈbetə ðən ˈfetʃɪŋ ˈslɪpəz ən(d) ˈfaɪndɪŋ ˈspektəklz¹⁷, ˈɪznt ɪt? (ˈraɪzɪŋ) baɪ ˈdʒɔːdʒ, ɪˈlaɪzə, aɪ ˈsed aɪd ˈmeɪk ə ˈwʊmən əv ˈjuː:; ən(d) aɪ ˈhæv. aɪ ˈlaɪk jʊ laɪk ˈðɪs.

---

¹ -rɪt ² pɔː ³ fɔːr ⁴ də, d ⁵ əˈnʌf ⁶ fjɔːrɪ ⁷ -jɪŋ ⁸ -nʊr- ⁹ də-, daɪ- ¹⁰ rə- ¹¹ -əlɪ ¹² ɪntʊ ɪz ¹³ əˈhɑː ¹⁴ bə- ¹⁵ -es ¹⁶ -bədɪ ¹⁷ -tɪk-

48 /θ/ AND /ð/ WORD PUZZLE

(For directions see p. 122)

At completion of the puzzle there will be no letters remaining.

Athene
author
bath
bathe
birth
blythe
bother
brother

cloth
clothes

earth

father
fathom

hath
health
heath

maths
method
month
moth
mother
myth

otherwise

paths
pithy

Ruth

seethe
south
southern
sympathy

thanks
that
the
thee
these
thick
think
this (2x)
thither (2x)
though
thorough
thunder
thus
thine

weather
with
worth

49

What is a hobbit? I suppose hobbits need some description nowadays, since they have become rare and shy of the Big People, as they call us. They are (or were) a little people, about half our height, and smaller than the bearded Dwarves. Hobbits have no beards. There is little or no magic about them, except the ordinary everyday sort which helps them to disappear quietly and quickly when large stupid folk like you and me come blundering along, making a noise like elephants which they can hear a mile off. They are inclined to be fat in the stomach; they dress in bright colours (chiefly green and yellow); wear no shoes, because their feet grow natural leathery soles and thick warm brown hair like the stuff on their heads (which is curly); have long clever brown fingers, good-natured faces, and laugh deep fruity laughs (especially after dinner, which they have twice a day when they can get it). Now you know enough to go on with.

J. R. R. Tolkien, *The Hobbit*

θ	ʌ	n	d	ə	θ	ð	ʌ	s	θ	p	s
l	ð	ɪ	a	l	b	uː	k	ʌ	ʴə	ɑː	ɪ
e	ə	θ	iː	n	iː	ŋ	r	ð	h	ð	m
h	w	e	ð	ə	æ	ə	ʌ	ə	æ	z	p
k	a	d	ə	θ	e	m	ʌ	n	θ	ə	ə
l	ɪ	n	ɪ	a	ð	æ	t	b	f	ð	θ
ə	z	ŋ	b	iː	ɔː	θ	ə	æ	ɒ	ɪ	ɪ
ʊ	k	ð	z	r	ɜː	ə	ð	ɑː	f	ð	iː
ð	l	ɪ	ə	w	ʌ	ə	ə	θ	iː	h	ə
z	ɒ	s	θ	æ	m	ð	ʊ	ɑː	ð	ɪ	w
ɪ	θ	ɪ	p	ɒ	iː	ɪ	ə	b	ɜː	θ	ɜː
s	a	ʊ	θ	s	ɪ	ð	θ	b	e	ɪ	ð

49

ˈwɒt ɪz[1] ə ˈhɒbɪt? aɪ s(ə)ˈpəʊz ˈhɒbɪts ˈniːd səm drˈskrɪpʃn̩ ˈnaʊədeɪz, sɪns ðeɪv bɪkʌm[2] ˈreər ən(d) ˈʃaɪ əv ðə ˈbɪg ˈpiːpl̩, əz ðeɪ ˈkɔːl əs. ðeɪ ˈɑː (ɔː ˈwɜː) ə ˈlɪtl̩ ˈpiːpl̩, əbaʊt ˈhɑːf aʊə[3] ˈhaɪt, ən(d) ˈsmɔːlə ðən ðə ˈbɪədɪd ˈdwɔːvz. ˈhɒbɪts hæv ˈnəʊ ˈbɪədz. ðər ɪz[4] ˈlɪtl̩ ɔː ˈnəʊ ˈmædʒɪk əˈbaʊt ðəm, ɪkˈsept[5] ðɪ ˈɔːd(ɪ)n(ə)rɪ[6] ˈevrɪdeɪ ˈsɔːt wɪtʃ ˈhelps ðəm tə dɪsəˈpɪə ˈkwaɪətlɪ ən(d) ˈkwɪklɪ wen ˈlɑːdʒ ˈstjuːpɪd ˈfəʊk laɪk ˈjuː ən(d) ˈmiː ˈkʌm ˈblʌnd(ə)rɪŋ əˈlɒŋ, ˈmeɪkɪŋ ə ˈnɔɪz laɪk ˈelɪfənts[7] wɪtʃ ðeɪ kən ˈhɪər ə ˈmaɪl ˈɒf. ðe(ɪ)ər ɪnˈklaɪnd[8] tə bɪ ˈfæt ɪn ðə ˈstʌmək; ðeɪ ˈdres ɪn ˈbraɪt ˈkʌləz (ˈtʃiːflɪ ˈgriːn ən(d) jeləʊ); weə ˈnəʊ ʃuːz, bɪkɒz[9] ðeə ˈfiːt grəʊ ˈnætʃ(ə)r(ə)l[10] ˈleðərɪ ˈsəʊlz ən(d) ˈθɪk ˈwɔːm braʊn ˈheə laɪk ðə ˈstʌf ɒn ðeə ˈhedz (wɪtʃ ɪz ˈkɜːlɪ); hæv ˈlɒŋ ˈklevə ˈbraʊn ˈfɪŋgəz, ˈgʊd-neɪtʃəd ˈfeɪsɪz, ən(d) lɑːf ˈdiːp ˈfruːtɪ ˈlɑːfs (ɪˈspeʃ(ə)lɪ[11] ɑːftə ˈdɪnə, wɪtʃ ðeɪ hæv ˈtwaɪs ə ˈdeɪ wen ðeɪ kən ˈget ɪt). ˈnaʊ jʊ nəʊ ɪˈnʌf[12] tə gəʊ ˈɒn ˈwɪð.

---

[1] wɒts [2] bə- [3] ɑː [4] ðəz [5] ek- [6] -d(ə)n- [7] elə- [8] ɪŋk- [9] bə-ˌbɪkəz [10] -tʃʊr- [11] esp- [12] əˈnʌʃ

129

50

The two creatures stood silent while I spoke, seeming to listen with great attention, and when I had ended they neighed frequently towards each other, as if they were engaged in conversation. I plainly observed that their language expressed the passions very well, and their words might with little pains be resolved into an alphabet more easily than the Chinese.
I could frequently distinguish the word Yahoo, which was repeated by each of them several times, and although it was impossible for me to conjecture what it meant, yet while the two horses were busy in conversation I endeavoured to practise this word upon my tongue, and as soon as they were silent I boldly pronounced Yahoo in a loud voice, imitating at the same time as near as I could the neighing of a horse, at which they were both visibly surprised, and the gray repeated the same word twice, as if he meant to teach me the right accent, wherein I spoke after him as well as I could, and found myself perceivably to improve every time, though very far from any degree of perfection. Then the bay tried me with a second word, much harder to be pronounced, but reducing it to the English orthography may be spelt thus, Houyhnhnms.

Jonathan Swift, *Gulliver's Travels*

51

All the world's a stage,
And all the men and women merely players:
They have their exits and their entrances;
And one man in his time plays many parts,
His acts being seven ages. At first the infant,
Mewling and puking in the nurse's arms.
And then the whining schoolboy, with his satchel,
And shining morning face, creeping like snail
Unwillingly to school. And then the lover,
Sighing like furnace, with a woeful ballad
Made to his mistress' eyebrow. Then a soldier,
Full of strange oaths, and bearded like the pard,
Jealous in honour, sudden and quick in quarrel,
Seeking the bubble reputation
Even in the cannon's mouth. And then the justice,
In fair round belly with good capon lin'd,
With eyes severe, and beard of formal cut,

50

ðə ˈtuː ˈkriːtʃəz stʊd ˈsailənt wail ai ˈspəʊk, ˈsiːmiŋ tə ˈlisn wið ˈgreit əˈtenʃn, ən(d) ˈwen ai (h)(ə)d ˈendid ðei ˈneid ˈfriːkwəntli t(ə)wɔːdz[1] ˈiːtʃ ˈʌðə, əz ˈif ðei wər inˈgeidʒd[2] in kɒnvəˈseiʃn. ai ˈpleinli əbˈzɜːvd ðət ðeə ˈlæŋgwidʒ ikˈsprest[3] ðə ˈpæʃnz ˈveri ˈwel, ən(d) ðeə ˈwɜːdz mait wið ˈlitl ˈpeinz bi riˈzɒlvd[4] intʊ ən ˈælfəbit[5] ˈmɔːr ˈiːzili ðən ðə tʃaiˈniːz.

ai kəd ˈfriːkwəntli diˈstiŋgwiʃ ðə ˈwɜːd jəˈhuː[6], witʃ wəz riˈpiːtid[4] bai ˈiːtʃ əv ðəm ˈsevr(ə)l ˈtaimz, ən(d) ɔːlˈðəʊ it wəz imˈpɒsəbl[7] fə mi tə kənˈdʒektʃə ˈwɒt it ˈment, jet ˈwail ðə ˈtuː ˈhɔːsiz wə ˈbizi in kɒnvəˈseiʃn ai inˈdevəd tə ˈpræktis ˈðis ˈwɜːd əpɒn[8] mai ˈtʌŋ, ən(d) əz ˈsuːn əz ðei wə ˈsailənt ai ˈbəʊldli prəˈnaʊnst[9] jəˈhuː[6] in ə ˈlaʊd ˈvɔis, ˈimiteitiŋ ət ðə ˈseim ˈtaim əz ˈniər əz ai ˈkʊd ðə ˈneiiŋ əv ə ˈhɔːs, ət ˈwitʃ ðei wə ˈbəʊθ ˈvizibli səˈpraizd, ən(d) ðə ˈgrei riˈpiːtid[4] ðə ˈseim wɜːd ˈtwais, əz ˈif (h)i ˈment tə ˈtiːtʃ mi ðə ˈrait ˈæks(ə)nt[10] weərin ai ˈspəʊk ˈɑːftə him[11] əz ˈwel əz ai ˈkʊd, ən(d) ˈfaʊnd maiself pəˈsiːvəbli[12] tʊ imˈpruːv ˈevri ˈtaim, ðəʊ ˈveri ˈfɑː frəm ˈeni diˈgriː: əv pəˈfekʃn. ˈðen ðə ˈbei ˈtraid mi wið ə ˈsek(ə)nd ˈwɜːd, ˈmʌtʃ ˈhɑːdə tə bi prəˈnaʊnst[9], bət riˈdjuːsiŋ[4] it tə ði ˈiŋ(g)liʃ ɔːˈθɒgrəfi mei bi spelt ˈðʌs, ˈhʊi(h)n(ə)mz[13].

[1] tʊ-, tɔːdz   [2] iŋ-, en-   [3] eks-   [4] rə-   [5] -bet   [6] jɑː-   [7] -ibl   [8] -ən   [9] prʊ-   [10] -ent   [11] ɑftər im   [12] pɜː-   [13] hʊˈin(ə)mz

51

ˈɔːl ðə ˈwɜːldz ə ˈsteidʒ,
ən(d) ˈɔːl ðə ˈmen ən(d) ˈwimin ˈmiəli ˈpleiəz:
ðei ˈhæv ðeər ˈeksits[1] ən(d) ðeər ˈentrənsiz;
ən(d) ˈwʌn ˈmæn in (h)iz ˈtaim pleiz ˈmeni ˈpɑːts,
hiz ˈækts biːiŋ ˈsevn ˈeidʒiz. ət ˈfɜːst ði ˈinfənt,
ˈmjuːliŋ ən(d) ˈpjuːkiŋ in ðə ˈnɜːsiz ˈɑːmz.
ən(d) ˈðen ðə ˈwainiŋ ˈskuːlbɔi, wið (h)iz ˈsætʃ(ə)l,
ən(d) ˈʃainiŋ ˈmɔːniŋ ˈfeis, ˈkriːpiŋ laik ˈsneil
ʌnˈwiliŋli tə ˈskuːl. ən(d) ˈðen ðə ˈlʌvə,
ˈsaiiŋ laik ˈfɜːnis[2], wið ə ˈwəʊf(ʊ)l ˈbæləd
ˈmeid tə hiz[3] ˈmistris[2] ˈaibraʊ. ˈðen ə ˈsəʊldʒə[4],
ˈfʊl əv strein(d)ʒ ˈəʊðz[5], ən(d) ˈbiədid ˈlaik ðə ˈpɑːd,
ˈdʒeləs in ˈɒnə, ˈsʌdn ən(d) ˈkwik in ˈkwɒr(ə)l,
ˈsiːkiŋ ðə ˈbʌbl repjʊˈteiʃn[6]
ˈiːvn in ðə ˈkænənz ˈmaʊθ. ən(d) ˈðen ðə ˈdʒʌstis,
in ˈfeə raʊnd ˈbeli wið gʊd ˈkeipən ˈlaind,
wið ˈaiz siˈviə[7], ən(d) ˈbiəd əv ˈfɔːml ˈkʌt,

[1] egz-   [2] -əs   [3] tʊ iz   [4] -djə   [5] -θs   [6] -pju: [7] sə-

Full of wise saws and modern instances;
And so he plays his part. The sixth age shifts
Into the lean and slipper'd pantaloon,
With spectacles on nose and pouch on side,
His youthful hose well sav'd a world too wide
For his shrunk shank; and his big manly voice,
Turning again towards childish treble, pipes
And whistles in his sound. Last scene of all,
That ends this strange eventful history,
Is second childishness, and mere oblivion,
Sans teeth, sans eyes, sans taste, sans everything.

William Shakespeare, *As You Like It*

52 BRITISH PLACENAMES

Identify the places from their clues and enter their phonetic transcription in the list, writing one phoneme per space. The fact that a specific number represents the same phoneme throughout the list will help you in completing the puzzle.

1. Tomb of St. Cuthbert
2. Second largest English city
3. Welsh Abertawe
4. City near Scottish border
5. Cathedral collection of OE poems
6. City on the Thames
7. African city has same name
8. Pirates of . . .
9. City on the Severn
10. Last landfall of "Mayflower"
11. Famous horseraces
12. U.S. President had same name
13. Seaport in Essex
14. Bodleian Library
15. Cutlery manufacture
16. Seaside resort
17. Channel Island
18. Famous soccer team
19. Famous meat sauce
20. Oscar Wilde imprisoned here
21. Burial place of Richard III
22. Wordsworth lived here
23. Famous for marmalade
24. Burial place of Lewis Carrol
25. Home of the "Beatles"
26. University founded in 1209
27. Birthplace of the Bard
28. Birthplace of C. S. Lewis
29. Famous pilgrimage site
30. National Library of Wales

ˈfʊl əv waɪz ˈsɔːz ən(d) ˈmɒd(ə)n ˈɪnstənsɪz;
ən(d) ˈsəʊ (h)ɪ ˈpleɪz (h)ɪz ˈpɑːt. ðə ˈsɪksθ eɪdʒ ˈʃɪfts
ɪntə ðə ˈliːn ən(d) ˈslɪpəd pæntəˈluːn,
wɪð ˈspektəklz ɒn ˈnəʊz ən(d) ˈpaʊtʃ ɒn ˈsaɪd,
hɪz ˈjuːθf(ʊ)l ˈhəʊz wel ˈseɪvd ə ˈwɜːld tuː ˈwaɪd
fə hɪz[8] ˈʃrʌŋk ˈʃæŋk; ən(d) (h)ɪz ˈbɪg ˈmænlɪ ˈvɔɪs,
ˈtɜːnɪŋ əˈgeɪ(ɪ)n t(w)ɔːdz ˈtʃaɪldɪʃ ˈtrebl, ˈpaɪps
ən(d) ˈwɪslz ɪn (h)ɪz ˈsaʊnd. ˈlɑːst siːn əv ˈɔːl,
ðət ˈendz ðɪs ˈstreɪn(d)ʒ ɪˈventf(ʊ)l ˈhɪst(ə)rɪ,
ɪz ˈsek(ə)nd ˈtʃaɪldɪʃnɪs[2], ən(d) ˈmɪər əbˈlɪvɪən[9]
sænz ˈtiːθ, sænz ˈaɪz, sænz ˈteɪst, sænz ˈevrɪθɪŋ.

---

[8] fər ɪz [9] ɒb-, -vjən

Stresses in this passage have been marked to show an expressive reading of the text rather than to indicate the typical scansion of iambic pentameter (blank verse).

1. $\overline{27}\ \overline{5}\ \overline{7}\ \overline{10}\ \overline{25}$
2. $\overline{36}\ \overline{30}\ \overline{25}\ \overline{14}\ \overline{37}\ \overline{10}\ \overline{25}$
3. $\overline{18}\ \overline{33}\ \overline{1}\ \overline{8}\ \overline{6}\ \overline{14}$
4. $\overline{21}\ \overline{29}\ \overline{13}\ \overline{34}\ \overline{13}$
5. $\overline{16}\ \overline{21}\ \overline{18}\ \overline{14}\ \overline{19}\ \overline{10}$
6. $\overline{13}\ \overline{5}\ \overline{8}\ \overline{27}\ \overline{10}\ \overline{8}$
7. $\overline{18}\ \overline{26}\ \overline{13}\ \overline{6}\ \overline{36}\ \overline{10}\ \overline{7}\ \overline{14}$
8. $\overline{2}\ \overline{16}\ \overline{8}\ \overline{6}\ \overline{3}\ \overline{8}\ \overline{18}$
9. $\overline{32}\ \overline{13}\ \overline{1}\ \overline{18}\ \overline{19}\ \overline{10}$
10. $\overline{2}\ \overline{13}\ \overline{14}\ \overline{25}\ \overline{10}\ \overline{22}$
11. $\overline{27}\ \overline{29}\ \overline{36}\ \overline{14}$
12. $\overline{13}\ \overline{14}\ \overline{37}\ \overline{21}\ \overline{10}\ \overline{8}$
13. $\overline{23}\ \overline{3}\ \overline{7}\ \overline{14}\ \overline{44}$
14. $\overline{1}\ \overline{21}\ \overline{18}\ \overline{17}\ \overline{10}\ \overline{27}$
15. $\overline{12}\ \overline{16}\ \overline{17}\ \overline{39}\ \overline{13}\ \overline{27}$
16. $\overline{36}\ \overline{26}\ \overline{8}\ \overline{25}\ \overline{10}\ \overline{22}$
17. $\overline{32}\ \overline{30}\ \overline{8}\ \overline{6}\ \overline{14}$
18. $\overline{13}\ \overline{39}\ \overline{27}\ \overline{6}$
19. $\overline{33}\ \overline{40}\ \overline{18}\ \overline{19}\ \overline{10}$
20. $\overline{7}\ \overline{16}\ \overline{27}\ \overline{14}\ \overline{37}$
21. $\overline{13}\ \overline{16}\ \overline{18}\ \overline{19}\ \overline{10}$
22. $\overline{32}\ \overline{7}\ \overline{29}\ \overline{18}\ \overline{25}\ \overline{9}$
23. $\overline{27}\ \overline{5}\ \overline{8}\ \overline{27}\ \overline{39}$
24. $\overline{32}\ \overline{14}\ \overline{13}\ \overline{17}\ \overline{10}\ \overline{27}$
25. $\overline{13}\ \overline{14}\ \overline{31}\ \overline{10}\ \overline{2}\ \overline{24}\ \overline{13}$
26. $\overline{21}\ \overline{11}\ \overline{25}\ \overline{36}\ \overline{7}\ \overline{14}\ \overline{44}$
27. $\overline{18}\ \overline{19}\ \overline{7}\ \overline{3}\ \overline{19}\ \overline{17}\ \overline{10}\ \overline{27}$
28. $\overline{36}\ \overline{16}\ \overline{13}\ \overline{17}\ \overline{29}\ \overline{18}\ \overline{19}$
29. $\overline{21}\ \overline{3}\ \overline{8}\ \overline{19}\ \overline{10}\ \overline{36}\ \overline{10}\ \overline{7}\ \overline{14}$
30. $\overline{3}\ \overline{36}\ \overline{10}\ \overline{7}\ \overline{14}\ \overline{18}\ \overline{19}\ \overline{33}\ \overline{14}\ \overline{22}$

53

East Cheam Public Library. Tony enters, carrying a pile of books. He goes up to the Librarian's desk and puts them down.

Tony: Good morrow, good curator.

Librarian: Oh it's you. Overdue again. Seven reminders I've sent out to you.

Tony: My dear good fellow one cannot rush one's savouring of the classics of world literature. Rome wasn't built in a day, and its decline and fall can't be read in one.

Librarian: You haven't got Gibbon's *Decline and Fall* there.

Tony: That's got nothing to do with it. I've got the love lives of the Caesars here, that tells me everything . . . and between you and me, I'm not surprised it declined and fell after that lot. Kindly shove the cards back in the sockets and give me the tickets.

The Librarian goes through the books and looks inside the covers.

Librarian: How have you got all these books? How many tickets have you got?

Tony: Two fiction and two non-fiction.

Librarian: That's four tickets. There's ten books here.

Tony: Yes well, Dolly was on last time.

Librarian: Do you mean Miss Hargreaves?

Tony: She may be Miss Hargreaves to you, but to people who she reckons she is Dolly. And to me she is Dolly. And she always lets me have a few over the odds.

Librarian: That's three and eight to pay on this lot.

Tony: Three and eight? I don't want to buy 'em.

Librarian: Well don't take so many books out if you can't read them all in time. There are other people who want to borrow these books you know.

Tony: I can't think why. A bigger load of old rubbish I haven't clapped my reading glasses on in years.

Librarian: Then why did you take them out?

Tony: Well there's not much choice here, is there? I suppose Lolita's still out.

Librarian: Yes.

Tony: I thought so.

R. Galton/A. Simpson, *Hancock's Half Hour*

ˈiːst ˈtʃiːm ˈpʌblɪk ˈlaɪbr(ə)rɪ. ˈtəʊnɪ ˈentəz, ˈkærɪɪŋ ə ˈpaɪl əv ˈbʊks. hɪ gəʊz ˈʌp tə ðə laɪˈbreərɪənz desk ən(d) ˈpʊts ðəm ˈdaʊn.

ˈtəʊnɪ: gʊd ˈmɒrəʊ, ˈgʊd kjʊ(ə)ˈreɪtə.

laɪˈbreərɪən: ˈəʊ, ɪts ˈjuː. ˈəʊvədjuː əˈge(ɪ)n. ˈsevn rɪˈmaɪndəz[1] aɪv ˈsent ˈaʊt tə ˈjuː.

ˈtəʊnɪ: maɪ ˈdɪə gʊd ˈfeləʊ, wʌn ˈkænɒt ˈrʌʃ wʌnz ˈseɪv(ə)rɪŋ əv ðə ˈklæsɪks əv ˈwɜːld ˈlɪt(ə)rətʃə[2]. ˈrəʊm wɒznt ˈbɪlt ɪn ə ˈdeɪ, ən(d) ɪts dɪˈklaɪn ən(d) ˈfɔːl ˈkɑːnt bɪ ˈred ɪn ˈwʌn.

laɪˈbreərɪən: jʊ ˈhævnt gɒt ˈgɪbənz dɪˈklaɪn ən(d) ˈfɔːl ðɛə.

ˈtəʊnɪ: ˈðæts gɒt ˈnʌθɪŋ tə ˈduː wɪð ɪt. aɪv gɒt ðə ˈlʌv ˈlaɪvz əv ðə ˈsiːzəz ˈhɪə, ˈðæt ˈtelz mɪ ˈevrɪθɪŋ . . . ən(d) bɪˈtwiːn[3] ˈjuː ən(d) ˈmiː, aɪm ˈnɒt səˈpraɪzd ɪt dɪˈklaɪnd ən(d) ˈfel ɑːftə ˈðæt ˈlɒt. ˈkaɪndlɪ ˈʃʌv ðə ˈkɑːdz ˈbæk ɪn ðə ˈsɒkɪts ən(d) ˈgɪv mɪ ðə ˈtɪkɪts.

ðə laɪˈbreərɪən ˈgəʊz θruː ðə ˈbʊks ən(d) ˈlʊks ɪnˈsaɪd ðə ˈkʌvəz.

laɪˈbreərɪən: ˈhaʊ (h)(ə)v jʊ ˈgɒt ˈɔːl ðiːz ˈbʊks? ˈhaʊ menɪ ˈtɪkɪts (h)əv jʊ ˈgɒt?

ˈtəʊnɪ: ˈtuː ˈfɪkʃn ən(d) ˈtuː ˈnɒn fɪkʃn.

laɪˈbreərɪən: ˈðæts ˈfɔː ˈtɪkɪts. ðəz ˈten ˈbʊks hɪə.

ˈtəʊnɪ: ˈjes ˈwel, ˈdɒlɪ wəz ˈɒn ˈlɑːst taɪm.

laɪˈbreərɪən: djʊ ˈmiːn mɪs ˈhɑːgriːvz?

ˈtəʊnɪ: ʃɪ ˈmeɪ bɪ mɪs ˈhɑːgriːvz tə ˈjuː, bət tə ˈpiːpl (h)ʊ ʃɪ ˈrek(ə)nz ʃiːz ˈdɒlɪ. ən(d) tə ˈmiː ʃiːz ˈdɒlɪ. ən(d) ʃiː ˈɔːlweɪ(ɪ)z[4] ˈlets mɪ ˈhæv ə ˈfjuː ˈəʊvə ðɪ ˈɒdz.

laɪˈbreərɪən: ˈðæts ˈθriː ən(d) ˈeɪt tə ˈpeɪ ɒn ˈðɪs ˈlɒt.

ˈtəʊnɪ: ˈθriː ən(d) ˈeɪt? aɪ ˈdəʊnt ˈwɒnt tə ˈbaɪ əm.

laɪˈbreərɪən: wel ˈdəʊnt ˈteɪk səʊ menɪ bʊks ˈaʊt ɪf jʊ ˈkɑːnt ˈriːd ðəm ˈɔːl ɪn ˈtaɪm. ðər ər ˈʌðə ˈpiːpl hʊ ˈwɒnt tə ˈbɒrəʊ ˈðiːz ˈbʊks, jʊ ˈnəʊ.

ˈtəʊnɪ: aɪ ˈkɑːnt θɪŋk ˈwaɪ. ə ˈbɪgə ˈləʊd əv əʊld ˈrʌbɪʃ aɪ ˈhævnt ˈklæpt maɪ ˈriːdɪŋ ˈglɑːsɪz ˈɒn ɪn ˈjɜːz[5].

laɪˈbreərɪən: ðen ˈwaɪ dɪdʒʊ[6] ˈteɪk ðəm ˈaʊt?

ˈtəʊnɪ: wel ðəz ˈnɒt mʌtʃ ˈtʃɔɪs hɪə, ˈɪz ðɛə? aɪ s(ə)ˈpəʊz lə ˈliːtəz ˈstɪl ˈaʊt.

laɪˈbreərɪən: ˈjes.

ˈtəʊnɪ: aɪ ˈθɔːt səʊ.

---

[1] rə- [2] -rɪtʃə, -tjʊə [3] bə- [4] -wəz [5] jɪəz [6] jʊ

54

It is sometimes suggested that the terminology, or 'jargon', of modern linguistics is unnecessarily complex. This is a criticism which need not detain us long. Every science has its own technical vocabulary: it is only because the layman takes on trust the established sciences, and especially the 'natural' sciences, that he does not question their right to furnish themselves with special vocabularies. The technical terms used by linguists arise in the course of their work and are easily understood by those who approach the subject sympathetically and without prejudice. It should not be forgotten that most of the terms which the non-linguist employs to talk about language ('word', 'syllable', 'letter', 'phrase', 'sentence', 'noun', 'verb', etc.) originated as technical terms of traditional grammar and are no less 'abstract' in their reference than the more recent creations of linguists. If the contemporary linguist requires different terms, instead of, or in addition to, those familiar to the layman, this is accounted for partly by the fact that the non-technical employment of many of the terms of traditional grammar has rendered them insufficiently precise for scientific purposes and partly by the simple fact that modern linguistics has in certain respects advanced beyond traditional grammar in its attempt to construct a general theory of language-structure.

John Lyons, *Introduction to Theoretical Linguistics*

55

Phonetics gathers raw material. Phonemics cooks it. Practical phonetics provides a technique for describing sounds in terms of movements of the vocal apparatus, and for writing them in terms of articulatory formulas, i.e. as letters of a phonetic alphabet. Practical phonemics provides a technique for processing the rough phonetic data in order to discover the pertinent units of sound.

Kenneth L. Pike, *Phonemics*

56

"Dear Sir, Kindly excuse John's absence from school yesterday afternoon, as he fell in the mud. By doing the same you will greatly oblige his mother."

ɪt ɪz ˈsʌmtaɪmz səˈdʒestɪd ðət ðə tɜːmɪˈnɒlədʒɪ, ɔː ˈdʒɑːɡən, əv ˈmɒdən lɪŋˈɡwɪstɪks ɪz ʌnˈnesəs(ə)rəlɪ[1] ˈkɒmpleks. ˈðɪs ɪz ə ˈkrɪtɪsɪzm wɪtʃ ˈniːd nɒt dɪˈteɪn əs ˈlɒŋ. ˈevrɪ ˈsaɪəns hæz ɪts ˈəʊn ˈteknɪkl və(ʊ)ˈkæbjʊlərɪ[2]: ɪt ɪz ˈəʊnlɪ bɪkɒz[3] ðə ˈleɪmən ˈteɪks ɒn ˈtrʌst ðɪ ɪˈstæblɪʃt[4] ˈsaɪənsɪz, ən(d) ˈɪspeʃ(ə)lɪ[4] ðə ˈnætʃ(ə)r(ə)l[5] ˈsaɪənsɪz, ðət (h)ɪ ˈdʌznt ˈkwestʃn ðeə ˈraɪt tə ˈfɜːnɪʃ ðəmselvz wɪð ˈspeʃl və(ʊ)ˈkæbjʊlərɪz[2]. ðə ˈteknɪkl ˈtɜːmz ˈjuːzd baɪ ˈlɪŋɡwɪsts əˈraɪz ɪn ðə ˈkɔːs əv ðeə ˈwɜːk ən(d) ər ˈiːzɪlɪ[6] ʌndəˈstʊd baɪ ˈðəʊz hu əˈpraʊtʃ ðə ˈsʌbdʒɪkt[7] sɪmpəˈθetɪk(ə)lɪ ən(d) wɪˈðaʊt ˈpredʒʊdɪs[8]. ɪt ˈʃʊdnt bɪ fəˈɡɒtn ðət ˈməʊst əv ðə ˈtɜːmz wɪtʃ ðə ˈnɒn-ˈlɪŋɡwɪst ɪmˈplɔɪz[9] tə ˈtɔːk əbaʊt ˈlæŋɡwɪdʒ (ˈwɜːd, ˈsɪləbl, ˈletə, ˈfreɪz, ˈsentəns, ˈnaʊn, ˈvɜːb, ɪtˈset(ə)rə)[10] əˈrɪdʒəneɪtɪd[11] əz ˈteknɪkl ˈtɜːmz əv trəˈdɪʃ(ə)n(ə)l ˈɡræmər ən(d) ə ˈnəʊ ˈles ˈæbstrækt ɪn ðeə ˈref(ə)r(ə)ns ðən ðə ˈmɔː ˈriːsnt kriːˈeɪʃnz[12] əv ˈlɪŋɡwɪsts. ɪf ðə kənˈtemp(ə)rərɪ ˈlɪŋɡwɪst rɪˈkwaɪəz[13] ˈdɪf(ə)r(ə)nt ˈtɜːmz, ɪnˈsted ˈɒv, ɔːr ɪn əˈdɪʃn ˈtʊ[14], ˈðəʊz fəˈmɪljə[15] tə ðə ˈleɪmən, ˈðɪs ɪz əˈkaʊntɪd ˈfɔː: ˈpɑːtlɪ baɪ ðə ˈfækt ðət ðə ˈnɒn-ˈteknɪkl ɪmˈplɔɪmənt[9] əv menɪ əv ðə ˈtɜːmz əv trəˈdɪʃ(ə)n(ə)l ˈɡræmə[16] həz ˈrendəd ðəm ɪnsəˈfɪʃntlɪ prɪˈsaɪs[17] fə saɪənˈtɪfɪk ˈpɜːpəsɪz ən(d) ˈpɑːtlɪ baɪ ðə ˈsɪmpl ˈfækt ðət ˈmɒdən lɪŋˈɡwɪstɪks (h)əz ɪn ˈsɜːtn rɪˈspekts[13] ədˈvɑːnst brˈjɒnd[18] trəˈdɪʃ(ə)n(ə)l ˈɡræmər ɪn ɪts əˈtem(p)t tə kənˈstrʌkt ə ˈdʒen(ə)r(ə)l ˈθɪərɪ əv ˈlæŋɡwɪdʒ-ˈstrʌktʃə.

[1] -sɪs-, -ser-, ˌʌnnesəˈser-, -ɪlɪ [2] vʊk-, -bjəl- [3] bə-, -kəz [4] es- [5] -tʃʊr- [6] -əlɪ [7] -ekt [8] dʒə- [9] em- [10] et-, ət- [11] ɒr-, -dʒɪn- [12] krɪ- [13] rə- [14] tuː [15] -lɪə [16] ɡræmər əz [17] prə- [18] bɪˈɒnd

fə(ʊ)ˈnetɪks ɡæðəz ˈrɔː məˈtɪərɪəl. fə(ʊ)ˈniːmɪks ˈkʊks ɪt. ˈpræktɪkl fə(ʊ)ˈnetɪks prəˈvaɪdz[1] ə tekˈniːk fə dɪˈskraɪbɪŋ ˈsaʊndz ɪn tɜːmz əv ˈmuːvmənts əv ðə ˈvəʊkl æpəˈreɪtəs, ən(d) fə ˈraɪtɪŋ ðəm ɪn tɜːmz əv ɑːˈtɪkjʊlət(ə)rɪ[2] ˈfɔːmjʊləz[3], aɪ ˈiː[4] əz ˈletəz əv ə fə(ʊ)ˈnetɪk ˈælfəbɪt[5]. ˈpræktɪkl fə(ʊ)ˈniːmɪks prəˈvaɪdz[1] ə tekˈniːk fə ˈprəʊsesɪŋ[6] ðə ˈrʌf fə(ʊ)ˈnetɪk ˈdeɪtə[7] ɪn ɔːdə tə dɪˈskʌvə ðə ˈpɜːtɪnənt ˈjuːnɪts əv ˈsaʊnd.

[1] prʊ- [2] -leɪt- [3] -jəl- [4] ðæt ɪz [5] -bet [6] -sɪs- [7] dɑːtə

ˈdɪə ˈsɜː, ˈkaɪndlɪ ɪkˈskjuːz[1] ˈdʒɒnz ˈæbs(ə)ns frəm ˈskuːl ˈjest(ə)dɪ[2] ɑːftəˈnuːn, əz (h)ɪ ˈfel ɪn ðə ˈmʌd. baɪ ˈduːɪŋ ðə seɪm jʊ wɪl ˈɡreɪtlɪ əˈblaɪdʒ (h)ɪz ˈmʌðə.

[1] eks- [2] -deɪ

57 SOUNDS ON A STRING

Transcribe the following words into the puzzle. Words start at each number and follow the lines. At completion lines A to C will give a well-known proverb.

1 began	6 enquire
2 inedible	7 bushman
3 erred	8 than (WF)
4 Hindu	9 girth
5 these	10 hot

58

A distinction must be made between Standard English, which is a *dialect* in use by educated speakers of English throughout the world, and 'Received Pronunciation', which is the *accent* of English usually associated with a higher social or educational background, with the BBC and the professions, and that most commonly taught to students learning English as a foreign language. Many people speak unimpeachable Standard English as far as words and grammar are concerned, though with regional features in their pronunciation (accent). Like Standard English, however, RP owes its origin to educated London speech, which during the Middle Ages began to acquire social prestige and eventually changed from a regional to a class dialect. In England great prestige is still attached to this standard of pronunciation, which, throughout its history, has had a marked effect on the various regional forms of pronunciation. Between RP and the dialects it is useful to distinguish the intermediate variety 'modified regional' as a type of pronunciation modified by the adoption of RP characteristics to a greater or lesser degree, e.g. the use of RP [ɑː] in *chaff, grass, path, dance,* instead of northern dialectal [a].

Martyn F. Wakelin, *English Dialects: An Introduction*

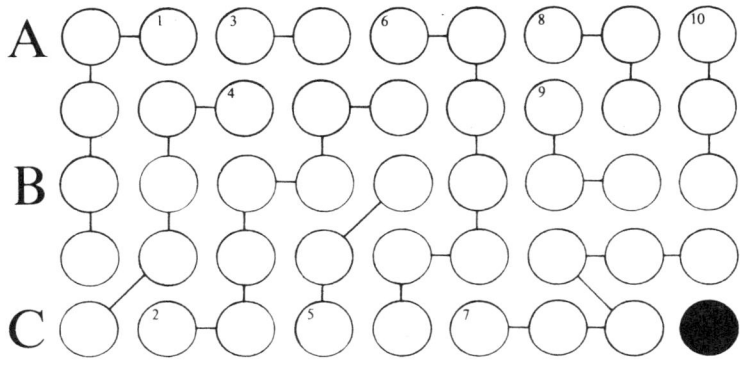

58

ə dɪˈstɪŋ(k)ʃn məs(t) bɪ ˈmeɪd bɪtwiːn[1] ˈstændəd ˈɪŋ(g)lɪʃ, wɪtʃ ɪz ə ˈdaɪəlekt ɪn ˈjuːs baɪ ˈedjuːkeɪtɪd[2] ˈspiːkəz əv ˈɪŋ(g)lɪʃ θruːˈaʊt[3] ðə ˈwɜːld, ən(d) rɪˈsiːvd[4] prənʌnsɪˈeɪʃn[5], wɪtʃ ɪz ði ˈæks(ə)nt[6] əv ˈɪŋ(g)lɪʃ ˈjuːʒ(ʊ)(ə)lɪ[7] əˈsəʊʃɪeɪtɪd[8] wɪð ə ˈhaɪə ˈsəʊʃl ɔːr edjuːˈkeɪʃ(ə)n(ə)l[2] ˈbækgraʊnd, wɪð ðə biː biː ˈsiː ən(d) ðə prəˈfeʃnz[5], ən(d) ˈðæt məʊs(t) ˈkɒmənlɪ ˈtɔːt tə ˈstjuːdnts ˈlɜːnɪŋ ˈɪŋ(g)lɪʃ əz ə ˈfɒrən[9] ˈlæŋgwɪdʒ. ˈmenɪ ˈpiːpl spiːk ʌnɪmˈpiːtʃəbl ˈstændəd ˈɪŋ(g)lɪʃ əz fɑːr əz ˈwɜːdz ən(d) ˈgræmər ə kənˈsɜːnd, ðəʊ wɪð ˈriːdʒ(ə)n(ə)l ˈfiːtʃəz ɪn ðeə prənʌnsɪˈeɪʃn[5] (ˈæks(ə)nt[6]). ˈlaɪk ˈstændəd ˈɪŋ(g)lɪʃ, haʊˈevə, ɑːˈpiː əʊz ɪts ˈɒrɪdʒɪn tʊ ˈedjuːkeɪtɪd[2] ˈlʌndən ˈspiːtʃ, wɪtʃ djʊərɪŋ[10] ðə ˈmɪdl ˈeɪdʒɪz bɪˈɡæn[1] tʊ əˈkwaɪə ˈsəʊʃl preˈstiːʒ ən(d) ɪˈventʃʊ(ə)lɪ[11] ˈtʃeɪn(d)ʒd frəm ə ˈriːdʒ(ə)n(ə)l tʊ ə ˈklɑːs ˈdaɪəlekt. ɪn ˈɪŋ(g)lənd ˈgreɪt preˈstiːʒ ɪz ˈstɪl əˈtætʃt tə ˈðɪs ˈstændəd əv prənʌnsɪˈeɪʃn[5], ˈwɪtʃ, θruːˈaʊt[3] ɪts ˈhɪst(ə)rɪ, həz hæd ə ˈmɑːkt ɪˈfekt ɒn ðə ˈveərɪəs ˈriːdʒ(ə)n(ə)l ˈfɔːmz əv prənʌnsɪˈeɪʃn[5]. brɪtwiːn[1] ɑːˈpiː ən(d) ðə ˈdaɪəlekts ɪt ɪz ˈjuːsf(ʊ)l tə dɪˈstɪŋgwɪʃ ði ɪntəˈmiːdjət[12] vəˈraɪətɪ ˈmɒdɪfaɪd ˈriːdʒ(ə)n(ə)l, əz ə ˈtaɪp əv prənʌnsɪˈeɪʃn[5] ˈmɒdɪfaɪd baɪ ði əˈdɒpʃn əv ɑːˈpiː kærəktəˈrɪstɪks[13] tʊ ə ˈgreɪtər ɔːˈlesə dɪˈgriː, fər ɪgˈzɑːmpl[14] ðə ˈjuːs əv ɑːˈpiː [ɑː] ɪn tʃɑːf, ˈɡrɑːs, ˈpɑːθ, ˈdɑːns, ɪnsted əv ˈnɔːðən daɪəˈlektl [a].

---

[1] bə- [2] edʒuː-, edjʊ-, edʒʊ- [3] θruː- [4] rə- [5] prʊ- [6] -sent [7] -ʒw(ə)lɪ [8] -əʊsɪ-, -əʊsj-, -əʊʃj- [9] -rɪn [10] djɔː-, dʒʊər-, dʒɔː- [11] -tjwəlɪ, -tjʊ(ə)lɪ, -tʃwəlɪ [12] -dɪət, -djɪt, -dɪt [13] -rɪk- [14] ˈiːˈdʒiː

59

Within RP itself it is convenient to distinguish three main types: the *conservative* RP forms used by the older generation and, traditionally, by certain professions or social groups; the *general* RP forms most commonly in use and typified by the pronunciation adopted by the BBC; and the *advanced* RP forms mainly used by young people of exclusive social groups—mostly of the upper classes, but also, for prestige value, in certain professional circles. In its most exaggerated variety, this last type would usually be judged 'affected' by other RP speakers, in the same way that all RP types are liable to be considered affected by those who use unmodified regional speech. Advanced pronunciations, however, whenever they are not the result of temporary fashion, may well indicate the way in which the RP system is developing and be adopted in the future as general RP, e.g. the originally advanced ('affected') diphthong in *home,* involving increased centralization and a tendency towards monophthongization, seems likely to become general in a very short time.

> A. C. Gimson,
> *An Introduction to the Pronunciation of English*

60

IT was decided almost two hundred years ago that English should be the language spoken in the United States. It is not known, however, why this decision has not been carried out.

> George Mikes, *How to Skrape Skies*

61

Humpty Dumpty sat on a wall,
Humpty Dumpty had a great fall.
All the king's horses,
And all the kings men,
Couldn't put Humpty together again.

59

wɪð'ɪn ɑː 'piː ɪt'self ɪt ɪz kən'viːnjənt[1] tə dɪ'stɪŋwɪʃ 'θriː 'meɪn 'taɪps: ðə kən'sɜːvətɪv 'ɑː piː 'fɔːmz 'juːzd baɪ ðɪ 'əʊldə dʒenə'reɪʃn ænd, trə'dɪʃ(ə)n(ə)lɪ, baɪ 'sɜːtn prə'feʃnz[2] ɔː 'səʊʃl 'gruːps; ðə 'dʒen(ə)r(ə)l 'ɑː piː 'fɔːmz məʊs(t) 'kɒmənlɪ ɪn 'juːs ən(d) 'tɪpɪfaɪd baɪ ðə prənʌnsɪ'eɪʃn[2] ə'dɒptɪd baɪ ðə biː biː 'siː; ən(d) ðɪ əd'vɑːnst 'ɑː piː 'fɔːmz 'meɪnlɪ 'juːzd baɪ 'jʌŋ 'piːpl əv ɪk'skluːsɪv[3] 'səʊʃl 'gruːps-'məʊs(t)lɪ əv ðɪ 'ʌpə 'klɑːsɪz, bət 'ɔːlsəʊ, fə pre'stiːʒ 'væljuː[4], ɪn 'sɜːtn prə'feʃ(ə)n(ə)l[2] 'sɜːklz. ɪn ɪts 'məʊst ɪg'zædʒəreɪtɪd[5] və'raɪətɪ, ðɪs 'lɑːs(t) 'taɪp wʊd 'juːʒ(ʊ)(ə)lɪ[6] bɪ 'dʒʌdʒd ə'fektɪd baɪ 'ʌðər 'ɑː piː 'spiːkəz, ɪn ðə 'seɪm 'weɪ ðət 'ɔːl ɑː 'piː 'taɪps ə 'laɪəbl tə bɪ kən'sɪdəd ə'fektɪd baɪ 'ðəʊz hʊ 'juːz 'ʌnmɒdɪfaɪd 'riːdʒ(ə)n(ə)l 'spiːtʃ. əd'vɑːnst prənʌnsɪ'eɪʃnz[2], haʊ'evə, wen'evə ðe(ɪ)ə 'nɒt ðə rɪ'zʌlt[7] əv 'temp(ə)rərɪ 'fæʃn, meɪ 'wel 'ɪndɪkeɪt ðə 'weɪ ɪn wɪtʃ ðɪ ɑː 'piː 'sɪstəm[8] ɪz dɪ'veləpɪŋ[9] ən(d) bɪ ə'dɒptɪd ɪn ðə 'fjuːtʃər əz 'dʒen(ə)r(ə)l 'ɑː piː:, fər ɪɡ'zɑːmpl[10] ðɪ ə'rɪdʒ(ə)n(ə)lɪ[11] əd'vɑːnst [ə'fektɪd] 'dɪfθɒŋ[12] ɪn 'həʊm, ɪnvɒlvɪŋ ɪn'krɪst sentr(ə)l(a)ɪ'zeɪʃn ən(d) ə 'tendənsɪ təwɔːdz[13] mɒnəfθɒŋg(a)ɪ'zeɪʃn, siːmz 'laɪklɪ tə bɪ'kʌm[14] 'dʒen(ə)r(ə)l ɪn ə 'verɪ 'ʃɔːt 'taɪm.

---

[1]-nɪənt [2] prʊ- [3] eks- [4] -jʊ [5] eɡz- [6] -w(ə)lɪ [7] rə- [8] -tɪm [9] də- [10] iː dʒiː [11] ɒr-, -dʒɪ- [12] dɪp- [13] tʊ-, twɔːdz, tɔːdz [14] bə-

60

ɪt wəz dɪ'saɪdɪd 'ɔːlməʊst[1] 'tuː 'hʌndrəd[2] 'jɜːz' ə'ɡəʊ ðət 'ɪŋ(g)lɪʃ ʃəd bɪ ðə 'læŋɡwɪdʒ 'spəʊk(ə)n ɪn ðə juː'naɪtɪd[4] 'steɪts. ɪt ɪz nɒt 'nəʊn, haʊ'evə, 'waɪ ðɪs dɪ'sɪʒn (h)əz 'nɒt bɪn 'kærɪd 'aʊt.

---

[1] ɒl-, -məst [2] -drɪd [3] jɪəz [4] jʊ-

61

'hʌm(p)tɪ 'dʌm(p)tɪ 'sæt ɒn ə 'wɔːl,
'hʌm(p)tɪ 'dʌm(p)tɪ 'hæd ə greɪt 'fɔːl.
'ɔːl ðə kɪŋz 'hɔːsɪz,
ən(d) 'ɔːl ðə kɪŋz 'men,
'kʊdnt pʊt 'hʌm(p)tɪ tə'geðər[1] ə'gen.

---

[1] tʊ-

62 HOMOPHONE PUZZLE

(For directions see p. 122)

A homophone of each of the following words is to be found within the puzzle diagram. The words occur in their orthographic version. At completion of the puzzle there will be no letters remaining.

air	Doug	law	side
alms		lie	some
	fare	low	sort
bare	fate		stares
be	feet	made	sure
bee	file		
Beatles	fought	oar	too
build		oh	
board	hay	or	wails
bore	here		weigh
bough	hi	pale	wen
boy	horde	pause	won
by	hymn		would
		rite	you
cane	kneel	sea	you'll
coal	kernel	sew	

63 PUZZLE SOLUTIONS

35

¹g	²r	³eɪ	⁴t	■	⁵s	⁶l	⁷ɪ	⁸m	⁹l	¹⁰ɪ
¹¹r	uː	l	■	¹²r	¹³eɪ	t	ɪ	n	j	uː z
¹⁴ɪ	n	k	¹⁵l	uː	d	ɪ	d	■	¹⁶uː	z
n	■	■	¹⁷e	θ	ɪ	k	■	¹⁸æ	z	■ ¹⁹æ
²⁰eɪ	²¹f	²²iː	t	■	²³ɪ	²⁴n	■	²⁵ɪ	²⁶m	p
²⁷ɪ	ə	z	■	²⁸eɪ	²⁹g	■	³⁰ɒ	³¹f	k	ɔː s
d	■	³²ɪ	³³l	■	³⁴r	³⁵ə	v	ɒ	l	t
■	³⁶ə	■	³⁷iː	d	ɪ	p	ə	s	■ ³⁸æ	³⁹d
⁴⁰b	l	⁴¹e	s	■	⁴²m	e	l	■ ⁴³iː	l	ɪ
⁴⁴l	aɪ	t	■	⁴⁵w	eɪ	t	■ ⁴⁶z	ɪ	p	
⁴⁷aɪ	k	■	⁴⁸e	ɪ	s	ɪ	⁴⁹s	t	■	■
⁵⁰ɪ	k	ə	r	ə	s	■ ⁵¹z	uː	m	ɪ	ŋ

39

¹s	²uː	²p	³ə	⁴s	⁵iː	⁶d	■	⁷d	e	⁸ɪ	⁹t
e	■ ¹⁰e	k	ɒ	l	ə	¹¹d	ʒ	ɪ	■	ɒ	
¹²s	p	r	ɪ	ŋ	■ ¹³m	e	ɪ	t	¹⁴ɪ	d	
ə	■ ¹⁵ɪ	n	■ ¹⁶s	ɜː	t	n	■ ¹⁷ə	m			
¹⁸m	¹⁹ɪ	l	■ ²⁰f	æ	r	ə	d	ɪ	■	ə	
²¹ɪ	n	■ ²²b	ɑː	l	ɪ	■	ʒ	■ ²³æ	d		
²⁴s	t	e	ɪ	■ ²⁶ɪ	ŋ	²⁷g	ə	²⁸t	■	ə	
²⁹t	ɜː	k	■	æ	n	■ ³⁰ɒ	r	ɪ	³²z	n	
r	■ ³³s	æ	n	d	■ ³⁴b	e	l	ɪ			
³⁵iː	³⁶t	■ ³⁷d	ʒ	e	l	ɪ	■ ³⁸ð	³⁹iː			
⁴⁰t	ʌ	n	d	r	ə	■ ⁴²ɪ	l	■ ⁴³ə	z		
■ ⁴⁴b	iː	■	uː	■ ⁴⁵ɒ	n	■ ⁴⁶iː	z	ɪ			

142

T	E	R	E	D	E	L	L	I	B	M	S
N	A	A	D	E	R	O	H	W	I	M	D
T	E	E	H	G	I	H	E	H	R	U	E
H	S	H	F	B	S	R	I	A	T	S	H
G	R	O	W	Ê	O	O	F	L	D	U	G
I	A	L	U	L	T	A	O	E	E	L	I
R	E	S	B	G	L	E	R	S	R	E	S
W	B	U	E	B	H	I	T	H	O	N	E
L	Y	E	S	E	L	T	E	E	B	O	W
F	A	I	R	H	I	Y	G	N	U	L	Y
A	E	E	U	M	A	I	D	I	O	O	U
T	W	O	O	D	P	W	W	A	Y	C	L
O	E	E	P	H	Y	L	E	C	O	L	E

63 PUZZLE SOLUTIONS

44

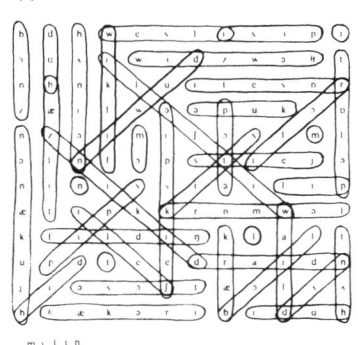

48

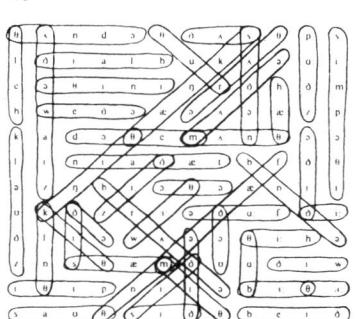

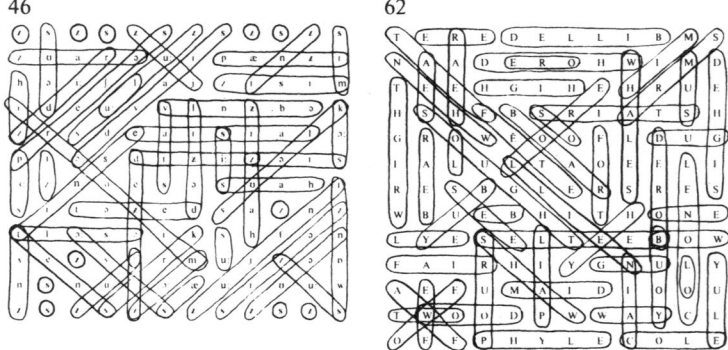

52

1. d ʌ r ə m
   27 5 7 10 25

2. b ɜː m ɪ ŋ ə m
   36 30 25 14 37 10 25

3. s w ɒ n zɪ ɪ
   18 33 1 8 6 14

4. k ɑː l aɪ l
   21 29 13 34 13

5. e k s ɪ t ə
   16 21 18 14 19 10

6. l ʌ n d ə n
   13 5 8 27 10 8

7. s ɔː l z b ə r ɪ
   18 26 13 6 36 10 7 14

8. p e n z æ n s
   2 16 8 6 3 8 18

9. ɡ l ɒ s t ə
   32 13 1 18 19 10

10. p l ɪ m ə θ
    2 13 14 25 10 22

11. d ɑː b ɪ
    27 29 36 14

12. l ɪ n k ə n
    13 14 37 21 10 8

13. h æ r ɪ dʒ
    23 3 7 14 44

14. ɒ k s f ə d
    1 21 18 17 10 27

15. ʃ e f iː l d
    12 16 17 39 13 27

16. b ɔː n m ə θ
    36 26 8 25 10 22

17. ɡ ɜː n z ɪ
    32 30 8 6 14

18. l iː d z
    13 39 27 6

19. w ʊ s t ə
    33 40 18 19 10

20. r e d ɪ ŋ
    7 16 27 14 37

21. l e s t ə
    13 16 18 19 10

22. ɡ r ɑː s m ɪə
    32 7 29 18 25 9

23. d ʌ n d iː
    27 5 8 27 39

24. ɡ ɪ l f ə d
    32 14 13 17 10 27

25. l ɪ v ə p uː l
    13 14 31 10 2 24 13

26. k eɪ m b r ɪ dʒ
    21 11 25 36 7 14 44

27. s t r æ t f ə d
    18 19 7 3 19 17 10 27

28. b e l f ɑː s t
    36 16 13 17 29 18 19

29. k æ n t ə b ə r ɪ
    21 3 8 19 10 36 10 7 14

30. æ b ə r ɪ s t w ɪ θ
    3 36 10 7 14 18 19 33 14 2

57

A ə—b—ɜː—d—ɪ—n—ð—ə—h
ɡ—ɪ—h—b—l—k—ɡ—n—ɒ
B æ—n—d—ɪ—z—w—ɜː—θ—t
n—d—e—iː—ɪ—a—m—ə—n
C uː—ɪ—n—ð—ə—b—ʊ—ʃ—●

A bird in the hand is worth two in the bush

ə bɜːd ɪn ðə hænd ɪz wɜːθ tuː ɪn ðə bʊʃ